THE MOBILIZATION FLYWHEEL

CREATING A CULTURE OF BIBLICAL MOBILIZATION

LARRY WALKEMEYER & TODD WILSON

WITH THANKS TO

An overwhelming debt of gratitude is owed to...

The team at Exponential, including Todd Wilson, Bill Couchenour, Terri Saliba, Brooks Hamon, Jason Stewart, Ralph Moore, Mariah Wilson, and Anna Wilson for their incredible servanthood to the church, the mission, and me.

Chad Harrington and his team at Harrington Interactive Media for contributing so much to this work with their masterful editing.

Karen Pheasant for her graphic and creative talent on the cover.

Ron Edmondson at Leadership Network for his input.

Light & Life Christian Fellowship whose devotion and sacrifice to be a multiplying church has helped me write books like these. I appreciate your prayers and support to do broader kingdom work like this. Thanks especially to our Executive Team of Pastors: Deb Walkemeyer, Sean Fenner, Joel Silva, and Ely Fournier, who cover so many bases to empower me to write.

A special thanks to my best friend since 1977, Deb Walkemeyer, who lives one of the most kingdom-centric, everyday missionary lives I have ever seen.

Most of all, I bless my Savior, Jesus Christ, whose mission I want to live and die for.

— LARRY WALKEMEYER

Featured Made for More Resources

MADE FOR MORE VISUAL GUIDE

This "read in an hour," visually engaging, resource introduces and integrates three new frameworks to help shift your ministry from a volunteer based *"we can do it, you can help"* approach to a *"you can do it, we can help"* missionary focused approach.

MORE

BE-DO-GO Framework

Who am I created to BE?
What am I made to DO?
Where am I to GO?

MADE FOR MORE BIBLE STUDY

The Six Shifts of Mobilization Framework

Bible study for staff & elders that highlights six key shifts that are necessary to create a healthy culture of mobilization.

THE MOBILIZATION FLYWHEEL

Church - Missionaries - Gathering Framework

Every person needs a healthy, biblical church family. Every believer is called and empowered to be an "everyday missionary." Gatherings can become new churches, strengthen existing churches or multiply themselves.

FREE downloads at exponential.org/ebooks.

ADDITIONAL MADE FOR MORE RESOURCES

Exponential and Made for More put together a large library of FREE Resources to go along with the 2019 theme Made for More: Mobilizing God's People, God's Way.

Additional Made for More Resources

- eBooks
    - *Made for More Bible Study*
    - *Made for More Devotional*
    - *Made for More Visual Guide*
    - *Millennials Calling*
    - *The Flywheel of Mobilization*
    - *Church Different*
    - More eBooks Coming!

- Made for More Resource Kits
    - Made for More Staff and Leadership Resource Kit
    - Made for More Personal Calling Kit

- Made for More On-Line Course

- Articles & Blog Posts (A collection of blog posts on Mobilizing God's People, God's Way.)

- Video Training (An exclusive video teaching series on how you can help mobilize every Christian into their calling to make disciples where they live, work, learn and play.)

- Audio Podcasts (a series of compelling conversations with some of today's most trusted voices on their personal calling.)

- Made for More Assessment Tool (coming soon!)

For information about the 2019 Made for More theme and other FREE Made for More Resources, please visit our Made for More Resource Page: https://exponential.org/made-for-more-resources/.

INSIDE

INTRODUCTION

The Flywheel of Mobilization

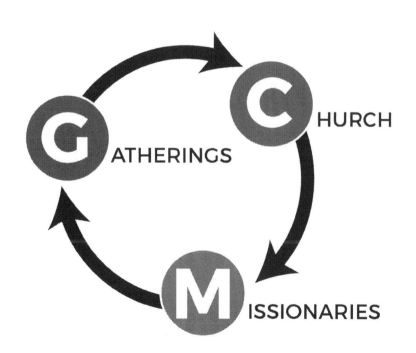

THE FLYWHEEL OF MOBILIZATION

In High School, I owned the fastest car of our small town in Kansas.[1] It was a 1969 Pontiac GTO, tricked out for drag racing, but I never raced it once. Instead I drove it slowly up and down Main Street listening to its beefy engine. All the power under the hood made a lot of noise but never did what it was created to do. My ultraconservative parents threatened to sell my car should they ever hear that I had raced it. My fear of losing the car kept me from racing the car.

When I reflect on the church in America, I think of my GTO. There seems to be much more noise than there is speed. We talk about the power and potential of the church, but we see disproportionate action compared to all the talk. The church and the individual Christians in her are missing their calling. That is, we have a mobilization deficiency.

The church has become fairly proficient at volunteer recruitment. So much so that **the church is the most effective volunteer mobilizer on the planet.** In fact, if you assigned a minimum hourly wage rate to all that volunteering, the result of those dollars would make the church one of the largest economies in the world.

Yet there's something about the whole volunteer system that feels "off," that feels like the potential of believers is being diminished to fit inside a restrictive "church box." Consequently, believers feel like they are gears in someone else's machine, instead of feeling like they're part of a mobilized force in God's mission.

The average church is always looking for more volunteers to do more church work. At the same time, the typical Christian is frequently seeking more purpose in their lives. Could the disconnect for both the church and the Christian be that they have missed the true meaning of "mobilization"?

> *mo·bi·lize* – 1) prepare and organize for active service, 2) make something movable or capable of movement[2]

Every believer and every church was made for more, made to be mobilized, made for "active service" in moving the kingdom of God forward in the world, made to help multiply the church.

This makes each of us in every church truly extraordinary!

John's Mobilization Story

My friend John was made for more. You wouldn't have guessed he was extraordinary, but he was. He was good at his job in computers, but he wasn't going to author the next groundbreaking software. He was simply faithful — faithful to his Lord, his wife, his family, his church, and his company.

But stirring inside of John's spirit was a holy discontent, an increasing yearning, a burgeoning spiritual imagination that somehow, he was *made for more.* John loved Jesus. He knew his purpose. He had a servant's heart, sat on the church board, and greeted at the church door. He was an exemplary church volunteer.

However, as he studied the leadership of Jesus, he wondered why the church's efforts didn't look more like the training and sending of the original disciples of Jesus. He observed that the church trained volunteers to pass out bulletins, while Jesus trained his disciples to cast out demons. He spoke up, then watched with interest as his church began to shift their ministry from a "consumer" mentality to a "sending" approach.

John, even though an introvert and more gifted as a teacher than an evangelist, kept hearing the call of Jesus to "GO" ... but he wasn't sure where to go. Then one day he and his wife felt the Lord saying, "Start where you are. I am sending you to your own neighborhood." Over the next weeks and months, they visited every home in their immediate area. Three people came to know Christ, many others were prayed for, and almost all were glad for the visit.

Next John stepped it up a notch and told his new neighborhood friends that he and his wife were starting a weekly gathering to laugh, eat, share, and discuss a Bible passage. Soon a lively group was meeting on a weekly basis at John's place and spiritual life was happening. John was still volunteering in his church, but his ministry passion was his unique neighborhood-based mission field.

Some of his group started attending his church, others went to other churches, and some found their fellowship in the weekly group meetings. Eventually John and his wife felt called to start a church, and as they were preparing to do so, a nearby church needed a pastor. John jumped in.

Today John leads a healthy church known for sending its members as missionaries into their neighborhoods. They are planning to start another church soon. I am incredibly blessed and inspired by John. To me, he's one type of hero in the mobilization stories God seeks to write.

Unfortunately, John's story is atypical — yet God desires stories like this to become normative. If we are going to reach our nation with the gospel, stories like John's must become the expected reality. We must begin to spin the mobilization flywheel and send the believers into the harvest field.

The Sent Ones

Isn't this what Jesus declared to his followers?

Jesus showed up behind locked doors on Resurrection Sunday evening to utter one of the most transformative pronouncements ever declared: "As the Father has *sent* me, I am *sending* you" (John 20:21).

If you had a recently deceased friend — imagine this with me — who suddenly showed up in ghost-like form to you in your bedroom, looked you in the eyes, and said, "Here's your mission, friend: Go do what you watched me do while I was alive," my guess is you would respond, "Yes, sir!"

The disciples should not have been surprised by Jesus' first resurrection declaration to them. After all, his *first* call to them in Matthew 4:19 was, "Follow me and I will *send* you out to fish for people." He was completing the loop. From start to finish, the call of discipleship is *to be sent*, to live as *sent ones*, to live *mobilized*!

When Jesus was sharing his prayer requests with the disciples, his primary request was "to *send* out workers into his harvest field" (Matt. 9:38). This was top of mind for Jesus.

The first disciples of Jesus would have been familiar with the call of the great prophet Isaiah. God's timeless, universal, yet personal question to us is the same one he asked Isaiah, "Whom shall I *send*? And who will go for us?" (Isa. 6:8).

It was a "mobilization" question. Isaiah was already in the temple. God's presence was there. He was doing good work *in* the temple. But there was a higher calling: to be *sent* ... and *from* the temple too! Isaiah heard God's question and with little understanding of what may transpire, responded with surrender, faith, courage, and adventure — "Here am I. *Send* me!" (Isa. 6:8, KJV).

We don't need pillars to shake, incense to smoke, and temples filled with God's glory to hear the "*sending* voice" of God. As Peter tells us, "We have also a more sure word of prophecy" (2 Pet. 1:19, KJV) declaring that being a believer means we are *"sent."* It is this *"sentness"* that is a crucial distinction of every true Christ-follower.

The Church in America Today

The church in America has largely missed this mobilization call. The church has mostly lived a "COME and SEE" model while Jesus operated from a "GO and BE" model.

If elements of God's mission can be compared to a football game, we might say that the focus has become the *huddle* instead of the line of scrimmage. The line of scrimmage is where the action happens. We have prioritized huddling over playing our part on the line of scrimmage by purchasing fancier uniforms for the huddle, composing cooler songs for the huddle, writing more speeches to inspire the huddle, positioning every person in the perfect spot for the huddle, holding conferences on how to build a better huddle, and even getting the perfect brew to pass around the huddle.

But Jesus' commission for the church was about *going*, not huddling. The huddle is vital, but it's only a brief moment to receive the playing directions from the quarterback. If you stay in the huddle too long, you get penalized and moved backward. The church is getting shoved backward on the mission field, and we point our finger at the enemy, but the problem is an overemphasis on the huddle. The church must be mobilized, it must be *sent* to the scrimmage line.

Our discontent screams that the church and its people are designed and *made for more.*

We believe that the pent-up, latent capacity of Christians who've never discovered and engaged their unique purpose and calling can become an unstoppable movement for good. If only we embrace our calling for more.

Made for More: BE, DO, GO

In my book *More: Find Your Personal Calling and Live Life to the Fullest Measure,* I (Todd) introduce the destiny blueprint God has for every Christian. It is a framework captured in three key words: BE, DO, GO. The three big questions in our lives are:

- Who am I created to BE?

- What am I made to DO?

- Where am I created to GO?

As you explore God's Word, all three questions are clearly answered: We are called to BE a child of God and a disciple of Jesus. The core mission we are sent to DO is make disciples. Our core position is to GO to the opportunities right where we are today. Together, these comprise the primary call of all Christians.

There is also, however, a secondary call that is unique to every individual. This call is revealed in Ephesians 2:10: "For we are God's masterpiece. He has created us anew in Christ Jesus, so we can do the good things he planned for us long ago" (NLT).

This passage says that we are uniquely made to do good works and deeds where we can be most effective. It can be describe as "your personal sweet spot." We have a one-of-a-kind design that distinguishes us from all other Christians. We have a unique purpose assigned to us by God that produces good works in our lives. We also have a distinctive position in which we can be the most effective.

> Read more on this in *More: Find Your Personal Calling and Live Life to the Fullest Measure* by Todd Wilson.

God's invitation is for us to explore opportunities as we listen for his voice directing us into his unique sweet spots for our lives.

When we become deeply engaged in our personal BE-DO-GO process, we make ourselves available to be "mobilized" or "sent." Rather than filling the slot with the most need in our church's ministry, we need to be asking the Spirit for clarity on our specific mission: Is there a more personalized mission God has for me that I am missing due to busyness or lack of seeking? Imagine the impact of releasing a movement of people mobilized in God's unique calling for their lives!

The Missing Bridge

So what's holding us back? We are not putting relational disciple-making Jesus' way as the core purpose of the church. The consequences? We don't champion the primary calling of individuals to be disciples who make disciples where they are. We embrace addition and accumulation-based measures of success instead of mobilization and multiplication. We take a pragmatic approach that values "COME, SEE, and STAY" (accumulation) versus "BE, DO, and GO" (mobilization). "COME, SEE, and STAY" is an approach that values what happens on the platform and in our services far above what happens throughout the week in the ordinary places of life. "BE, DO, and GO" prioritizes the equipping and sending of everyday missionaries even if it limits their church program involvement.

Too often we see individuals as volunteers to fuel our programs and to serve our purposes rather than as everyday missionaries with everyday mission fields — where they work, live, and play — that also provide the opportunity to accomplish God's purposes. As a result, we don't equip individuals to discover and live into their unique secondary calling.

Mobilization is the missing bridge between disciple-making and multiplication movements. With less than one percent of the churches ever multiplying, it is obvious we have a serious mobilization problem. It's the bridge of mobilization that's missing.

Our mobilization problem starts with change in the hearts and minds of Church leaders:

1. Our accumulation-based operating systems must change

2. Our personal and church scorecards of success must change

3. Our programmatic approach to adding disciples must be replaced with Jesus' style of relational disciple-making

Overall, leaders must shift from a bias of "*We* can do it, you can help" to one of "*You* can do it; how can we help?"

The Six Shifts of Ephesians

Just as there are essential paradigm shifts in our individual thinking, there are necessary shifts in the thinking and practice of the church. Paul's letter to the church in Ephesus reveals truths we need to embrace and shifts we need to make.

These six truths and shifts can be articulated this way:

phesians 1 – We need to embrace the truth and mystery that the fullness of Jesus can fill every corner of society through the church (vv. 15, 22-23).

→ We must shift our culture from more effort to more Jesus.

Ephesians 2 – We need to embrace the truth that every follower of Jesus is a masterpiece work of God with both a general and a unique calling (v. 10).

→ We must shift our culture from seeing people as volunteers to seeing them as unique masterpieces with a mission.

Ephesians 3 – We need to embrace the truth that our primary motivation for mobilization is love (v. 17-19).

→ We must shift our culture from more guilt to more love.

Ephesians 4 – We need to embrace the truth that our organizational structures should equip and deploy everyday missionaries (vv.11-16).

→ We must shift our culture from professional clergy doing the work of ministry to equipping and deploying everyday missionaries.

Ephesians 5 – We need to embrace the truth that our primary mission field is outside the walls of the church (vv. 15-16).

→ We must shift our culture from a program-based "COME and SEE" to a disciple-making "GO and BE" approach.

Ephesians 6 – We need to embrace the truth that we will face spiritual opposition when seeking to mobilize God's people, God's way (vv. 10-17).

To explore these shifts in much more detail, please see *Made for More Resource Kit* by Todd Wilson and Rob Wegner.

→ We must shift our culture from more strategy to more prayer, fasting, and surrender.

We have often misread a key text from Ephesians that casts the vision of mobilization: "And he gave the apostles, the prophets, the evangelists, the shepherds and teachers, to equip the saints for the work of ministry, for building up the body of Christ" (Eph. 4:11-12, ESV). Our equipping has focused on helping church people do church work within the church.

However, if you consider the form of the church in the first century, you quickly realize the ministry roles for work within the church were quite limited. There were no church buildings, no bulletins to print and pass out, no ushers, nurseries, children's ministries, youth ministries, worship bands, security teams, parking teams, no newsletters ... and no (gasp) church boards. Consequently, the "equipping" work the church leaders were doing was helping Christ followers evangelize and make disciples. The church leaders were mobilizing believers to be everyday missionaries!

The Flywheel of Mobilization

From merging personal calling with the essential shifts in the church, we can formulate a simple and powerful framework we call the "flywheel of mobilization." Although "flywheel" doesn't appear in Ephesians, Paul teaches the concepts of this analogy throughout the letter. Plus, they are demonstrated in Acts.

If this "flywheel" approach is understood and implemented, it can dramatically impact the church. For those unfamiliar with a "flywheel," the term comes from the world of mechanics:

> **Flywheel** — A heavy revolving wheel in a machine which is used to increase the machine's momentum and thereby provide greater stability or a reserve of available power.[3]

The flywheel is difficult to turn at first, requiring extra focus and energy. It must turn against the position of rest, the status quo, inertia. The flywheel first turns slowly but begins to acquire increased momentum with each revolution until it is not only easily turning but actually increasing the momentum and power.

Jim Collins employed the dynamics of the flywheel to popularize a concept he called the "flywheel effect" in the seminal business book *Good to Great*. On his website about this topic, Collins writes:

> No matter how dramatic the end result, good-to-great transformations never happen in one fell swoop. In building a great company or social sector enterprise, there is no single defining action, no grand

program, no one killer innovation, no solitary lucky break, no miracle moment. Rather, the process resembles relentlessly pushing a giant, heavy flywheel, turn upon turn, building momentum until a point of breakthrough, and beyond.[4]

Most Christian leaders want another Pentecost from heaven where they suddenly get to preach to thousands. But they aren't very interested in turning the flywheel of a movement, which takes daily discipleship effort. Leaders want a magic wand, not a flywheel.

After the miraculous day of Pentecost, however, the new church had to live out its mission to take the gospel to the world. God could have chosen to accomplish this mission in many miraculous ways — continued mass evangelism, large public churches in every city, an organized church hierarchy with a detailed strategic plan, an infiltration into the Roman political structure, or amazing public miracles — but instead God chose to do it person by person, disciple by disciple, group by group, church by church.

The flywheel of God's people started turning with Christ until it became a multiplication revolution:

- The apostles of Jesus began discipling the new converts who were saved at Pentecost.

- The apostles formed groups with these disciples from house to house (Acts 2:46) then organized these groups into the church, establishing elders such as James, the brother of Jesus.

- These churches became the equipping and launching place for *all* the disciples to carry out their "Jesus mission" in their distinctive personal mission fields.

The flywheel began turning.

Revival or Revolution?

True revival is a gift from God, but it is not emphasized in the New Testament. There are no directions given for how to start a revival. Praying for "revival" is admirable unless it causes the daily labor of evangelism, discipleship, starting groups, and planting churches to seem unremarkable, pedestrian, and ordinary. Daily faithfulness is what God most uses to build his kingdom.

In addition, most so-called "revivals" these days prioritize greater sensations *for* the saved, instead of greater sending *of* the saved. The "revival" we need is one that brings a "revolution" in the way we do church. This is the primary "revival" we see in international places where the gospel is spreading quickly. We need a revolution that arises from God's people being mobilized God's way, a revolution of more revolutions of what we're calling the "flywheel of mobilization."

The mobilization flywheel gains more power and momentum with each turn, leading to a more and more mobilized church. But unlike a simple mechanical flywheel, this spiritual flywheel also creates new flywheels as new churches are spun off and enter into this same dynamic process.

This mobilization flywheel arises from seven truths we sincerely believe:

1. Every person needs a healthy, biblical church family.

2. Every church should equip and send believers into their unique mission fields.

3. Every believer is called and empowered to be an "everyday missionary" to their unique mission field.

4. Most "everyday missionaries" can convene faith-based gatherings, and all missionaries can play a role in gatherings.

5. All gatherings can become new churches, strengthen existing churches, or multiply themselves.

6. Every church needs a clear understanding of what constitutes a biblical church.

7. Every church needs a family, network, or tribe as a connection beyond itself.

When each of these seven truths becomes operational, a flywheel is created and begins to spin. With each revolution, more energy and power is produced and more momentum is built. Flywheels can be used to produce energy that is converted to light to push back the darkness and revolutionize city streets.

In 2011, Massachusetts-based Beacon Power began serving the New York state electrical grid with the nation's largest flywheel plant. The 200 flywheels provide enough energy to meet about 10 percent of the state's daily needs.[5]

We dream of hundreds of churches that become mobilization flywheels, creating ever-increasing spiritual light that fills into every dark nook and cranny of society. Where does this start? According to Ephesians, it starts with the church.

CHAPTER 1

The Church: The Mobilization Starting Point

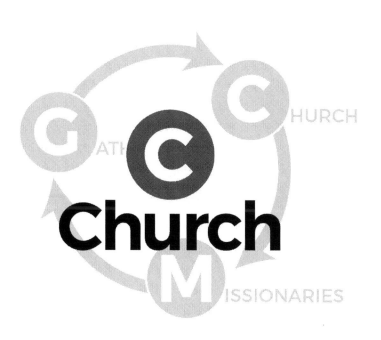

THE CHURCH

The first element of the mobilization flywheel is the church. Every believer needs and deserves a God-honoring, biblical church that embraces and practices its calling to equip and send everyday missionaries into everyday mission fields where they work, live, and play.

If we're going to get the mobilization flywheel to begin spinning toward revolution, it begins with the church because the church largely determines:

1. How believers see themselves

2. What believers expect of themselves and one another

3. What believers are trained to do

4. What believers are commissioned into

5. What believers celebrate and consequently repeat

With so much on the line, it is vital that churches understand their true calling.

> ### Building the Mobilization Flywheel:
>
> **100% of churches can become mobilization stations that equip and send believers.**

The church is both the starting point and the destination for the mobilization of believers.

The church sends the disciples out to build the church up.

The Building Project

Jesus only promised to build one thing on earth — his church! That's what he meant in Matthew 16:18 when he said, "On this rock I will build my church."

Jesus invites us into partnership with him in this eternal building project. Consider how we can:

- Be sure of our legacy when we have built his church on the rock of Christ.

- Build castles on the sand or churches on the rock.

- Encourage what the crowd applauds or what God applauds.

- See our mission in life as a quest to build a comfortable life for ourselves or as an adventure to co-labor with God to build his church for his glory.

- Pursue our selfish building plans or God's primary and secondary callings on our lives.

The apostle Peter unveils our calling both individually and corporately in 1 Peter 2:4-5:

> As you come to him, the living Stone — rejected by humans but chosen by God and precious to him — you also, like living stones, are being built into a spiritual house to be a holy priesthood, offering spiritual sacrifices acceptable to God through Jesus Christ.

The rock of Matthew 16:18 is the same as the living stone in 1 Peter 2:4. This rock of Christ is *the* Living Stone. We believers are "living stones," each built on the cornerstone. As we surrender individually to the Lordship of Jesus and collectively unite in our callings, we become "a spiritual house" — the church of Jesus. We each have our role in the building of this house. Old Testament priests were those who brought people far from God near to God. Correspondingly, we each become a part of this "holy priesthood," bringing the living stone to dying people.

The apostle Paul takes this metaphor further when he writes, "If I am delayed, you will know how people ought to conduct themselves in God's household, which is the church of the living God, the pillar and foundation of the truth" (1 Tim. 3:15). The church is God's "household," his tribe, his family. The church is where God chooses to make his "home" on earth. You might say that the name of Jesus is on the mailbox in front of his household.

We must start at God's house to reach those not yet inside his house.

Therefore, the first component of the mobilization flywheel is the church. To be more specific, it is the local church, which is a local family of believers, a local body of disciples. The church is the body of Christ, inseparable from the head, who is Christ.

The Church as a Mother and Family

There are an increasing number of people who, having viewed the excesses and abuses in the church, have tossed aside the church. Jesus might still be interesting to them, but the church is not. While this sentiment is somewhat understandable, this is not an available option. Those who want Jesus but not the church, are deceived to believe they can guillotine Christ from his body and keep only the head.

The church, however, is an essential partner in the process of people being "born again." Once "alive in Christ" the church acts as a parent to rear the child to maturity. Spiritual authorities throughout church history have underlined this truth for us. For example:

Cyprian of Carthage in 251 A.D. famously declared, "You cannot have God for your father unless you have the Church for your mother. If you could escape outside Noah's ark, you could escape outside the Church."[6] While Cyprian's application may seem extreme, there was an essential truth in his declaration.

Calvin echoed this truth that the church is necessary for all believers. He stated with regard to the church, "Let us learn even from the simple title 'mother,' how useful, indeed how necessary, it is that we should know her."[7]

Luther uses similar language in his *Large Catechism*: "Outside the Christian Church, that is, where the Gospel is not, there is no forgiveness, and hence no holiness ... The church is the mother that begets and bears every Christian through the word of God."[8]

Just as every child needs a parent so every Christian needs a church. We are born again not only into Christ but into his family, the church.

The church is a spiritual home for:

- Receiving and giving love
- Comforting and challenging one another
- Discovering and discerning God's truth together

- Being impacted by the gifts of one another

- Submitting to God's anointed leaders and learning their ways of life

- Operating on mission together

- Being sent *by* the family to *extend* the family

This spiritual family of the church is God's embracing and empowering gift to every believer.

Recently a notorious former gang member — who had come to Christ at Light & Life in Long Beach where I pastor and had been with us for a few years — came to me after service. In a voice hoarse with emotion, he exclaimed, "Pastor, this is the real family I was looking for when I joined my gang."

I replied, "It's the real family *everyone* is looking for."

In the church, we all find the family of God, and through the church, God begins to release the energy that spins the mobilization flywheel!

The Biblical, Eternal Church

Everyone who receives the new life of Christ deserves a community of faith that meets the biblical qualifications of a church. It is as a convert takes their place in the family that their new life of faith begins to grow. If we as believers provide "less than" the church (e.g., a loving group but not a biblical church) then we rob the new believer of the treasure Christ died to provide (more on this in Chapter 6).

The church is God's instrument for both the maturation and multiplication of the saints, for both the edification and the extension of the believers. God himself is the designer and initiator of this divinely created organism. It is an idea and entity which will last throughout eternity.

Paul's stunning prayer in Ephesians 3 ends with this blessing for all of us who will take hold of it by faith — *"to him be glory in the church and in Christ Jesus throughout all generations, for ever and ever! Amen"* (Eph. 3:21). It brings to the mind the closing doxology of the Lord's prayer (not in the scriptural text but dating to the *Didache* of the second century): "For thine is the kingdom, and the power, and the glory, forever. Amen." There is a "forever" dimension to God's kingdom being manifest through the church throughout endless ages.

The church will not only bring God glory throughout eternity, she will bring Him glory *now* through carrying out her mission. I love the Greek word *nyn* in Ephesians 3:10, which carries a meaning in English that's something like "at this present time, right now." The church is the communicator through her existence, her teachings, her actions of this beautiful, multi-colored (manifold) wisdom of God. It must profoundly irk the "rulers and authorities in the heavenly realms" that "now [*nyn*], through the church, the manifold wisdom of God should be made known" (Eph. 3:10).

Did you really catch what Ephesians 3:10 said? God's unfathomable plan involves taking fallen earthen vessels like us, binding us together as a family called "the church," then using us to carry the wisdom of the gospel to the world.

The church is indeed God's starting point for spinning of the mobilization flywheel.

The Church as the River

Ezekiel 47 contains one of the most powerful metaphors of the mobilizing church. In this passage, the prophet Ezekiel sees the temple, and there is water trickling from the south side of it. But then the trickle becomes a brook, then a stream, then a small river, then a powerful deep river that can not be crossed.

When Ezekiel views the temple, he does not see a lake — a place that collects and holds water.

Instead, he sees this holy river that grows the further it flows from the temple. The water brings life, abundance, fruitfulness and transformation. Ezekiel 47:9 tells us, "Where the river flows everything will live."

If we block the river inside the temple, the water stagnates. Yet this is a picture of much of the American church, the *immobilized church*. We try to collect and contain the water in one place around one pastor to grow larger lakes. In doing so, though, we miss Ezekiel's river.

In 1999, Light & Life was a fast-growing church. Many pointed to our church as an example of how urban, multi-ethnic churches can succeed in the city. God was indeed doing important ministry *in* our church. We just didn't have a vision for God doing important ministry *through* our church. Specifically, I didn't have a vision for "giving away" leaders and workers through mobilization. I wanted to be the biggest "lake" around, not a "river" or even a "trickle."

God's temple, however, is to be a sending place, a fountainhead of life, a flowing river, a force of power that turns the mobilization flywheel!

But this is where pastors grow reluctant and pushback starts: Pastors have a grip on their people. They want them to stay put so they will help fund and build the local church where they are. But what if pastors could start sending people into their mission fields with a vision to see them reach people, to disciple people, and to start groups and new churches?

Then it began. Our church began to prioritize "sending over keeping," and God released a "river" of life through us. Our thirty-nine parking spaces were no longer an imprisoning factor to us. We no longer pointed to those spaces as the problem but as the reason to be a river that pours into God's mission. As we began to send, God reached people through new ministries, groups, and churches that our local church as a "lake" could never have reached. We started helping people do what God had called them to do, rather than seeing them as assistants to help us build a bigger church. We had to change our operating system.

The Operating System of the Church

Every church has an "operating system," to use a tech term. The operating system of a church is the set of values a church is actually practicing on a weekly basis. A church's "operating system" must be both here *and* there.

It must be both a "family" caring for one another (here) and a "team" expecting mission accomplishment from one another (there). A healthy church practices:

1. Internal *and* external focus

2. Gathering *and* sending

3. Depending on one another *and* depending upon the spirit

4. Reaching consumers *and* making disciple-makers

5. Training in the classroom *and* training in the field

6. Reaching locally *and* reaching globally

The dominant operating system in the American church is built toward a consumer Christian.

A church architect was designing a new church building for a certain congregation. The architect asked the pastor, "What room needs to be largest in your new building?" The pastor replied, "If I was honest, I would have to say, 'the nursery' to hold all the baby Christians."

Too many pastors can relate.

The questions of how to attract, satisfy, entertain, retain, and monetize Christians to help "add to" our churches drive the prevailing operating system. Putting on the Sunday show demands a lot of motivated helpers.

Most churches in America have a "we can do it; you can help" operating system. New believers are enfolded into the church as volunteers in hopes they will help build the pastor's vision. Most of these churches have never planted another church, never sent a leader with group of believers to start a new gospel work in another part of the city or neighborhood.

A small minority of churches in America have a "*you* can do it; we can help" operating system. By this operating system, new believers are discipled and trained by asking, "What is God calling you to do and how can we help you live out that call?" Then the church assists them in discovering their strengths, gifts, talents, and calling. They are sent into their daily mission field. Their current day job is not something they need to leave for Jesus but something they can use for Jesus.

The difference between these two operating systems is like the difference between a golf match and a relay race. In a golf tournament, you want someone to carry your bag while you play the game. You want caddies who can do the grunt work and help you score.

In a relay, each runner gets to carry the baton and depends on the runner behind and ahead of them. Relay runners ask, "How can we help each other run our best race?" The team only wins the race if each one runs the portion assigned to them. But also, the most valuable part of the race is the baton. The baton is the mission of Christ himself and the mission must be carried all the way to the finish line. The critical portion of a relay race is the handoff of the mission so that the next runner is mobilized to do their assigned task. If the baton is dropped or mishandled, the race is lost. As Paul exhorts, the church must "run to win" (1 Cor. 1:24, NLT).

One defining Scripture for the church's operating systems that also illustrates this handoff of the baton is Ephesians 4:11-12: "So Christ himself gave the apostles, the prophets, the evangelists, the pastors and teachers, to equip his people for works of service, so that the body of Christ may be built up." Paul makes the call of the church clear: to be an equipping center.

This passage tells us this equipping happens:

1. Via the church

2. Through her variously gifted leaders/members

3. For the sake of ministry

4. Resulting in the building of the church

Until the American church majors in equipping and sending ordinary believers as missionaries, we will not see sustainable movements happening.

Rather than consuming nearly all the energy, time, and resources within the context of the church, a new breed of churches is needed — churches who major in mobilization.

The Operating System of Disciple-Making

This mobilization stems from biblical disciple-making. Biblical disciple-making must be the Operating System (OS) of the church. Let me tell you what mobilization is not:

- A new training curriculum the church implements

- A programmatic strategy which the church launches

- A small group model to be built

Instead, mobilization is rooted in disciple-making — a certain brand of disciple-making.

For too long the church's disciple-making process has revolved almost exclusively around the "Three C's" of content, character, caring:

- **Content** – If we can teach them enough of the Bible, they are discipled.

- **Character** – If we can help them become nicer people, they are discipled.

- **Caring** – If we can get them to help out in the church or serve in the community, they are discipled.

These "Three C's" are excellent but inadequate. From the beginning, biblical discipleship always majored in *going*. Disciples were sent to make other disciples. Increasing maturity was evidenced by increased spiritual activity by disciples among nonbelievers.

The missing "C" is "contagious": being so "infected" with Christ that others begin to catch what the believer has. Here's how we phrase this "C":

Contagious – If we can lead them to be disciple-makers themselves, they are discipled.

This is important for both individual believers and churches:

- **Biblical disciples** are individuals who have determined their most significant accomplishment in life will be making disciples who make disciples.

- **Biblical churches** are churches who have embraced an operating system that prioritizes and practices equipping and sending believers to be disciples who in turn make disciples in their unique mission fields.

When you survey current multiplying church movements globally and analyze multiplying church movements historically, you'll always find a clear emphasis on disciple-making that results in mobilization. Alan Hirsch has written that the operating system in the American church "is not built to produce disciples but rather to attract and retain religious consumers .... Every movement that changed the world had a primary emphasis on discipleship and disciple-making."[9]

The church will only see first century results when it uses first century methods.

Do you have a "gather and grow" or a "disciple and go" mindset in your church?

It is significant to observe that the first actual church building on record was built in the third century. If the early church was operating on a "gather and grow" model, it would have necessitated larger buildings dedicated to its purposes. But because the early church was functioning on a "disciple and go" model, it could multiply forward without facility constraints.

It is interesting to consider how the church in America might be impacted if all church buildings were outlawed. In order to understand how much of our method of "doing church" is built around the building, stop and contemplate how different Christianity in America would look without its buildings. Many church futurists who predict that this could be a reality soon. In a "disciple and go" model, however, the physical facility has little bearing upon the ministry effectiveness.

Today's church must retool its operating system with a mobilization bias.

The church must begin to have a "send, reach, go" mentality and priority:

- Churches must see themselves as equipping centers to send.
- Churches must see their people as missionaries who, when filled with the Spirit, can reach their world.
- Churches must commission their people with delegated authority to go in Jesus' name.

The ancient church meeting at Priscilla and Aquila's house understood this well.

Our Dream for the "Apolloses" of Today

When Apollos was brought into the fellowship at Priscilla and Aquila's, we are certain they were thrilled to have such a gifted, high-potential leader among them. Their priority, however, was not to consume his talents within their fellowship or even on their local mission. Instead, the leaders equipped Apollos (Acts 18:26) and undoubtedly encouraged him to listen for God's call on his life. Acts 18:27 tells us how the church responded when the Lord put Achaia on Apollos' heart: "When Apollos wanted to go to Achaia, the brothers and sisters encouraged him and wrote to the disciples there to welcome him."

The kingdom results are recorded in these words from Acts 18:27-28: "When he arrived, he was a great help to those who by grace had believed. For he vigorously refuted his Jewish opponents in public debate, proving from the Scriptures that Jesus was the Messiah."

As the pastor of a church-planting church, I can emotionally connect to what may have been happening in Ephesus. We will raise up a highly gifted leader, and my mind will begin to write plans for all the ways we can use the leader in our own context. It is tempting to influence the new leader to focus on our local church needs instead of listening to where God may be calling them. It's like I am wanting them to think "Ephesus" and forget "Achaia."

Is today's church so consumed with its Ephesus, it's missing its Achaia? Is today's church so possessive of its "Apolloses," it's discouraging them from going? Is today's church so pastor-centric that believers are motivated to climb upward in the church power structures instead of inspired to move outward into their mission fields?

CHAPTER 2

The Everyday Missionary: Mobilizing Believers

THE EVERYDAY MISSIONARY

When I was five years old, I traveled with my newly widowed mother to Africa. Although I was too young to realize the importance of what was happening, we were on a spiritual adventure. My aunt and uncle were serving as missionaries in a remote village in Burundi, and my twenty-eight-year-old mother was determined to visit them. For several weeks, we lived with them and experienced missionary ministry up close and personal.

God used that experience to shape my young heart and mind. To see two ordinary people courageously reach out in acts of service and words of truth was truly life-changing. A seed for missionary work was planted in me: I knew I wanted to be a missionary when I grew up.

One of my favorite memories is sitting on a log on top of a green hill surrounded by over 100 locals singing a chorus with them, "Everybody ought to know, everybody ought to know, who Jesus is: He's the lily of the valley. He's the bright and morning star. He's the fairest of ten thousand. Everybody ought to know."

I believe the truth of that song more than ever. But I've never lived internationally as a gospel worker. I have never been what most Christians think of when they say "missionary." But I have a new understanding of the word.

I am living on mission. I am seeking to courageously reach out in acts of service and words of truth to my Muslim neighbor from Egypt, my Vietnamese neighbor who is Buddhist, and my Canadian neighbor who is New Age. I am also trying to teach the believers in our church that they are "called" as "missionaries."

As the song we sang in Africa declared, "Everybody ought to know," but I don't believe they will know until everybody who is a believer starts functioning as an everyday missionary.

Until the church majors in equipping and sending ordinary believers as everyday missionaries, we're unlikely to see sustainable multiplication movements.

"The Missionary" defined: Believers acting upon their gifting, calling, and empowerment to reach their unique personal mission field. These are everyday missionaries bringing Jesus everywhere they live, work, and play.

The mobilization flywheel begins with churches who understand and implement their equipping and sending call. The flywheel moves forward as each believer embraces their personal calling from God and moves into their mission work:

> ### Building the Mobilization Flywheel:
>
> *100% of churches can become mobilization stations that equip and send believers.*
>
> **100% of believers have the calling and ability to be everyday missionaries where they live, work, or play.**

Ephesians 2:10 best frames this call of believers to be missionaries: "For we are God's handiwork, created in Christ Jesus to do good works, which God prepared in advance for us to do."

This is co-laboring with God — the individuality of the believer moving into the sovereignty of God's assignments for their lives. We were created physically by God but also created spiritually in Christ Jesus for the purpose of living on mission and accomplishing specific God-ordained tasks. Ephesians 2:10 declares every believer has a distinct calling to their own personal mission field. Since God prepared the mission beforehand for us, we can be certain he will be there with us. Our part is to hear God's call and obey.

My friend Marty Edwards was a disciple of Jesus before he became a fan of Harley-Davidsons. As Marty became a part of H.O.G (Harley Owners Group), he made friends and became burdened with God's heart for this subculture. As Marty continued to pray, he sensed God calling him to start discipling some of his new friends.

Soon a faith-based group, a small flock, was formed. Then God gave Marty a vision for a motorcycle ministry that would touch thousands of lives for Christ. Marty obeyed God's call. Marty's flock soon grew into a ministry called "Black Sheep – Harley-Davidson Riders for Christ." There are now chapters of this ministry in over forty states and different countries sharing the Good News and the great love of Jesus with those on two wheels. Marty is convinced this is one of the primary good works that God prepared in advance for him to do!

First Peter 2:9 echoes the truth about personal calling from Ephesians 2:10 in different words:

"But you are a chosen people, a royal priesthood, a holy nation, God's special possession, that you may declare the praises of him who called you out of darkness into his wonderful light."

This verse shows that the empowerment of each believer as part of the priesthood is for a divine purpose – to "*declare the praises*" and bring to the attention of others this great God who rescued them from darkness. Just a few verses later, 1 Peter 2:12 emphasizes the impact of each believer living out their "priestly identity" in their mission field: "Live such good lives among the pagans that, though they accuse you of doing wrong, they may see your good deeds and glorify God on the day he visits us" (1 Pet. 2:12).

The Christian celebrity culture is unintentionally undermining the priesthood of every believer. Creating a larger audience around and a growing dependency upon a centralized leader sends the opposite message. It inadvertently says, "I am the priest; you are not" or "You pay your tithe; I'll be your priest."

Our orthodoxy declares the priesthood of all believers, but our orthopraxy preaches a different truth. It is interesting that neither Jesus nor Paul, nor any of the apostles for that matter, were known by the size of their work but by the quality of their disciples. They were raising up a "new priesthood," which only had one "high priest." They were expecting priestly work from ordinary disciples — like my friend Charles Wallace.

The Starbucks Priest

Charles loved the Starbucks by his house. It was his "third place," his happy place, his thinking place, his social space — not to mention he loved their coffee. But about a year into his habit, he started hearing messages on "neighborhood and third-place missionaries." It dawned on him: he saw fifteen to twenty of the same people every day, and perhaps reaching this group was one of the good works God had planned for him in advance (Eph. 2:10). He started to pray and share his faith more boldly. The Starbucks folks started calling Charles "the Priest of Starbucks." Soon a few of his Starbucks friends had become followers of Jesus and were sharing with their friends. A multiplication chain had started.

Have you ever wondered how radically different 2 Timothy 2:2 would read if it had been written toward the "addition operating system" and celebrity culture we currently see in the church? It might read, *And the things you have heard me say in the presence of many witnesses, get excited about them and bring more people to hear them (especially reliable ones) and help those people invite others to come hear me too!*

Instead, 2 Timothy 2:2 says, "And the things you have heard me say in the presence of many witnesses entrust to reliable people who will also be qualified to teach others." The actual 2 Timothy 2:2 emphasizes the true definition and multiplication of disciple-making: empowering a believer to train another believer. The verse says, *You can do it; we can help!*

It says, *You can be a priest, too!*

The Multiplication Impact of Ordinary Missionaries

We have often heard pastors justify their ministry approach by appealing to the increased numbers of people who are now attending their services. We agree with their statement that Scripture cares about numbers because God cares about people; every number represents a person. This rationale is often used for affirming churches built on an over emphasis on the attractional model. We would suggest that the rationale is right, but the application is usually short-sighted.

The "numbers equals people" logic is precisely why discipleship, rather than attracting a crowd, is the focus in the New Testament. Attraction is good if the priority is on multiplication instead of addition. This means crowd size is a secondary concern while "the number in disciple-making training" must be primary. Multiplicative disciple-making will reach far more people over a decade than an attractional model.

It is why Jesus knew twelve multiplying disciples was a bigger number than 12,000 miracle seekers.

Latent in every ordinary Christian is a dynamic impact that would boggle their minds if implemented. Try telling an average Joe or Jane Jesus-follower that they could have a bigger ministry than a megachurch pastor, and see what type of reaction you get ... it'll probably be an exaggerated eye-roll of skepticism! The truth is that the most ordinary Christians can readily attain that size of influence through the multiplicative power of disciple-making.

The formula for this impact is straightforward:

Jesus' Method + Time + Faith = Exponential Kingdom Influence

Obviously, there are other elements, but that's the basic approach. Jesus discipled a handful of people over a three-year period, believing the Spirit would fill them and use them. Jesus' approach changed the world. We can copy it.

Consider this: If a disciple-maker invested in two other people for an entire year with one goal – to help them replicate what he or she was doing with them (i.e., make them disciple-makers). Then if each of the three of them did the same with two others the following year, and each of those six disciples spent a year making disciples of two others ... then by the end of just ten years over 39,000 disciples could be made. Even if attrition rates ran as high as 75 percent, over 10,000 disciples would exist because one ordinary believer reached out to their mission field with the methods of Jesus.

The Seventy-Two Unnamed Disciples

The anonymous seventy-two disciples in Luke 10 are prototypes for the church today. These seventy-two disciples were appointed, authorized, instructed, and sent by Jesus to certain towns and villages. They went in pairs, meaning thirty-six towns at once could be experiencing the kingdom power of Jesus, even though Jesus was not there in person.

These no-name disciples went in the power of Jesus' name. They proclaimed God's kingdom, cast out demons, healed the sick, and announced that Jesus would be coming soon. Then they joyfully returned to Jesus with their reports of how the kingdom had manifest itself through their mission. The seventy-two seemed astonished at what God could do through their faith. Jesus debriefed them, then used their experience to train them deeper in their kingdom work.

This story about the seventy-two creates anticipation for the type of ministry numerous unnamed believers can have: Jesus trained disciples to cast out demons, but we settle for training believers to pass out bulletins and wonder why the average Christian is bored. Now there's a place for "small" service, but there is a large gap between being a cog in someone else's ministry machine and growing your own garden. There is a vast difference between volunteers filling a space and ordinary missionaries reaching an unreached place.

Circles of Influence

In God's sovereignty, believers are *who* they are, *when* they are, and (to a degree) *where* they are by divine appointment. Our personalities, strengths, and inherited talents shape our calling. We were born into this generation, not the last one nor the next one. We currently live where we do based upon many circumstances, much of which we had no control over.

For the everyday missionary, this all means the Ephesians 2:10 "good works God planned for us" start where we are, not where we used to be or where hope to be. God has us where we are now to reach who lives there now.

We each have a "circle of influence": people you connect with through your neighborhood, work, school, third place, hobby, social group, family network, etc. Our immediate mission work for Jesus starts there, in your circle of influence. Fernando exemplifies this.

Fernando Cardiel was an ordinary believer faithfully attending and volunteering at our church. He was a greeter, an usher, and a church board member. He was also in management at a utility company. As we began to plant churches and preach the priesthood of all believers, Fernando began to wake up to his mission field, his calling, and the power of disciple-making multiplication. He determined God had given him his job for a reason — for the people who were already there. He began to share about his faith with different guys during lunch. Most weren't interested, but over a several-month period, three men received Christ. Fernando started to affectionately be known as "The Preacher." Fernando began discipleship training with the three guys he had reached. The effects of Fernando's ministry continue to create expanding ripples.

Even though being an individual missionary in a local context is of exceptional value, there are, woefully, very few "Fernandos." As lost people respond to the gospel, they can begin to be personally discipled *and* start looking for someone to disciple. This is the fulfilling of Jesus' Big Commission, "Go and make disciples." Sadly, this disciple-making work is an uncommon achievement.

Barna Research found in 2018 that seventy-six percent of churchgoers haven't heard of the Great Commission or can't remember what it means.[10] Even worse is Barna's finding that, "In 1993, 89 percent of Christians who had shared their faith agreed this is a responsibility of every Christian. Today, just 64 percent say so — a 25-point drop."[11]

An everyday missionary marches to an uncommon beat. For these normal (but tragically rare) disciples, the Great Commission is deeply understood and daily prioritized. They expect to be used by God on a daily basis to draw someone nearer to Christ.

What are some of the identifying marks of an "everyday missionary"? Even more, which ones are true of you?

Use these descriptions to think through those questions. An everyday missionary:

- Declares a circle of influence (mission field/unique context)
- Sees themselves as sent, a messenger and living ambassador of God to carry the fullness of Jesus to their unique context of influence
- Carries a burden and urgency for the lostness within their unique context of influence
- Sees and understands the people and needs around them and takes specific actions to meet needs within their unique context of influence
- Prays and fasts for the people and needs around them and for specific disciple-making opportunities
- Looks for opportunities to build relationships within their unique context of influence
- Looks for opportunities to engage in relational disciple-making

Let me share a story about everyday-missionary life. Although we are still growing into the everyday missionaries God wants us to be, we have seen some beautiful fruit. Some years ago, my wife, Deb, and I moved into a new rental house where the sixty-five-year-old owner lived behind us over the garage. The owner, Tracy, could see in our kitchen window and hear our occasional passionate discussions — my wife and I don't argue! — but also our frequent prayers. Deb began to intentionally reach out to Tracy with the gospel. I was admittedly reluctant at first, lest we create waves in the killer deal we had on the rent. But Deb believed God had moved us into that house to love Tracy into the kingdom. Deb had embraced her personal mission field, and she was right. Although it took a few years of prayer and sharing, Tracy committed to follow Jesus. Deb and I had the privilege of baptizing her. Tracy is family now and is active in our church family as well. These kind of everyday missionary stories can happen where you live, work, and play.

Discerning Your Circle of Influence

If you have ever had a negative multi-level sales experience, you can relate to this dirty little story from my distant past. I was recruited to make millions by selling little decorated cans of soil and seeds that were designed to be greeting cards/plants. They had wowed me with astounding statistics about the billions of dollars in the greeting card industry and assured me that I didn't really need to sell the cans, I just needed to convince other people to sell the cans; then I would just "can" a lot of money off their hard work.

The first thing my coach (think "sponsor," think "upline," think the guy who can make money off of me) did was have me list all the names of people I have known since preschool. After an hour of him pushing me to think broader, he looked at the list and declared that every one of them wanted to sell dirt in cans. He said these one hundred twenty-seven names were my "circle of influence" and I was about to make them rich! Three days and forty-two annoyed acquaintances later, I quit the job.

Unlike my "dirt can" sales experience, your circle of influence is not contrived or forced or meant to be manipulated, even though you really do want to make unbelievers wealthy (spiritually speaking). Your circle of influence is where you naturally interact with people, but now you become deeply burdened for them to awaken to the gospel.

Think about your circle of influence by asking yourself these questions:

- Where do I spend time with people on an ongoing basis?
- Where do I naturally connect with lost people?
- Where would I be considered a person of peace by an outsider?
- Where do I have a natural passion or burden for impact?
- Where can my unique calling be effectively utilized?
- What does God reveal to me through prayer and fasting?
- How does input or feedback from the people who know me best help?

Your everyday mission field is the place where your time, your potential relationships, your giftedness, your passions, and your burdens intersect.

Letting Your Light Shine

Think about some of the places your circle of influence has you. Where are some of the dark places that you bring the light of Jesus to?

The everyday mission fields look like:

- Neighborhood stay-at-home moms

- Players and parents on a youth sport's team

- Passengers on an airport shuttle bus

- Members at a local health club or gym

- Participants in a weekly hiking club

- Students in a school class

- Residents of a college dormitory

- Employees at a company

- Members of an online gaming community

Your mission field is where you do normal life activities. You are integrated into the "world" while influencing your world toward Christ. Light was made to transform darkness. A candle is not that significant in a light bulb factory. Salt is of little consequence resting safely inside a salt shaker with its fellow crystals. But candles lit in the pitch-black darkness of midnight become essential to navigating around. Salt shaken out changes what it touches.

Jesus uses these two examples, salt and light, before stating clearly: "In the same way, let your light shine before others, that they may see your good deeds and glorify your Father in heaven" (Matt. 5:16).

The "others" Jesus is talking here about are not those already in the church. The mobilization flywheel only begins to turn when it is outside the church. The church leaves the building when individual believers rise above simple church volunteerism to embrace their calling and awaken to their personal mission fields.

There is a huge difference between volunteers filling a space and everyday missionaries reaching a place.

Volunteers	Everyday Missionaries
Sacrifice their time, talent, and treasure to help a cause	Surrender to Jesus' calling on their life
Serve where they're needed, regardless of their gifting	Serve where they're gifted and called in their unique circle of influence
Schedule themselves to serve	See themselves as 24/7 servants

Most churches are using programs to teach people how to be disciples, then consuming their time by having them help with church ministries. The alternative is using equipped and mobilized everyday missionaries to do personal disciple-making as they make new disciple-makers.

Our program-driven approach to adding disciples produces an over reliance on volunteerism to fuel the internal operations of the church. This is one of the top tensions a church will face as it seeks to mobilize God's people, God's way.

Mobilizing Our Investments

As church leaders, we must shift our paradigm from recruiting volunteers to accomplish *"our thing"* to mobilizing everyday missionaries in their common and unique callings to accomplish *"God's thing."*

In Matthew's Gospel, the next-to-last story Jesus told is about a master who entrusted his three servants with varying amounts of money to manage and steward during his absence. Upon his return, the investments of his servants are analyzed.

The two who had invested by sending the money out to work for the master were given the following commendation: "Well done, good and faithful servant. You have been faithful over a little; I will set you over much. Enter into the joy of your master" (Matt. 25:21, ESV). Conversely, the servant who had fearfully hoarded the master's resources, keeping them hidden for himself, was rebuked for his lack of faith and his laziness.

As Christian leaders, our paramount resource is not our building, our bank account, our band, etc. ... it is the people the master has trusted us with leading. Stewardship starts in our minds with how we see people! They are far more than consumable resources. They are God's plan for carrying the fullness of Jesus into every nook and cranny of society.

We are called to be good stewards of God's handiwork and his provision in the form of his uniquely gifted and called people. When we shift our thinking from seeing people as "volunteers" who serve to "uniquely-made masterpieces with a purpose," we will more fully enter into our Master's joy! Everyday missionaries empowered, equipped — and equipped by churches who prioritize mobilization — will change their world. The flywheel is turning.

Questions to Consider

- Were you created for a significant spiritual purpose?

- Are you gifted by God to accomplish something important during your life?

- Do you believe you were saved for a mission on earth before departing for heaven?

- Were you given the Holy Spirit when you were born again? What does this make you capable of?

- Do you have a unique personality, signature talents, strengths, and specific spiritual gifts?

- Do you believe you are where you are by accident or by God's assignment?

- Do you believe God has called you to leave a legacy with your life?

- Is "going and making disciples" the highest call Jesus has given?

- Are you willing to engage your mission field with the gospel and make disciples?

CHAPTER 3

The Gathering: Mobilizing Groups

THE GATHERING

Charles and John Wesley started a faith-based gathering at Oxford College and began to reach out to classmates. In mockery, their fellow non-participating collegians began calling it the "Holy Club." The gathering was devoted to encouraging one another in devotion to God and service to those in need. *Christianity Today* says,

> The Holy Club never exceeded twenty-five members, but many of those made significant contributions, in addition to those of Charles and John Wesley. John Gambold later became a Moravian bishop. John Clayton became a distinguished Anglican churchman. James Hervey became a noted religious writer. Benjamin Ignham became a Yorkshire evangelist. Thomas Brougham became secretary of the SPCK. George Whitefield, who joined the club just before the Wesleys departed for Georgia, was associated both with the Great Awakening in America and the Evangelical Revival in England.[12]

Although perhaps an extraordinary example, the truth is gatherings have an inherent power to create significant movements. They power the flywheel to turn faster.

The Importance of Gatherings

What happens when an everyday missionary impacts their mission field?

Gatherings, of course! Jesus emphasized the influence and essentiality of gatherings: "Where two or three gather in my name, there am I with them" (Matt. 18:20).

I define a gathering as follows:

Gathering — A group of two or more people convened around faith, meeting together to discover and obey God's truths and purposes for their lives and in their world.

A gathering includes at least one function of a healthy church and puts priority on obedience-based disciple-making. Functions such as bible study, prayer, fellowship, accountability, service, worship, skill development, training, etc.

The mobilization flywheel turns forward with increasing measure as churches send missionaries who make disciples, then gathering them together into groups for kingdom purposes. These faith-based gatherings provide the community necessary for the gifts of the Spirit to begin to operate and create even more missional momentum.

Building the Mobilization Flywheel:
100% of churches can become mobilization stations that equip and send believers.
100% of believers have the calling and ability to be everyday missionaries where they live, work, or play.
100% of everyday missionaries can play a role in gatherings.
Most everyday missionaries can form and lead a gathering of seekers or believers.

Questions to Consider

- Did Jesus primarily make disciples one-on-one or in small groups?

- Can the "one another" passages of Scripture be done in solitude or in a large anonymous crowd?

- Does life change and spiritual growth happen best in the context of a small group of believers?

- Can small groups effectively assist believers in discovering their gifts, talents, and calling?

- Can you accomplish your calling without the help of others in the body of Christ?

- Does a small group on mission serve the needs of a local community better than solo Christians?

- Have some of your most memorable, meaningful times been with a small circle of friends?

The answers to the questions above decisively point us toward the paramount importance of the gatherings of the believers.

In this age of individualism when we interact almost solely through technology, gatherings are easily devalued or misunderstood. Allow me to describe a few important truths about gatherings:

Gatherings are natural. It's in our God-imparted design to come together in social circles.

> "The LORD God said, 'It is not good for the man to be alone. I will make a helper suitable for him'" (Gen. 2:18).

Gatherings were Jesus' method. Twelve disciples who were called, gathered, then sent.

> "He appointed twelve that they might be with Him and that He might send them out to preach" (Mark 3:14).

The example of Jesus was not primarily one-on-one discipleship. Rather, Jesus did his discipling in the context of smaller groups of disciples. Whether Jesus was working with The Three (Peter, James, John) or The Twelve or The Seventy-Two, he was gathering a group around his teaching and training them to repeat the pattern.

Gatherings were the early church's pattern. Disciples were baptized, gathered together in homes, and sent out to serve.

> "They broke bread in their homes and ate together with glad and sincere hearts, praising God and enjoying the favor of all the people. And the Lord added to their number daily those who were being saved" (Acts 2:46-47).

Gatherings were central to Paul's ministry approach. His approach was characterized by a patter: reaching some lost people, gathering people around their faith, teaching the believers, and leaving to start another.

> "You know that I have not hesitated to preach anything that would be helpful to you but have taught you publicly and from house to house" (Acts 20:20).

As everyday missionaries sent from the church to their world and beginning to reach individuals with the gospel, there opens the possibility of bringing them together in a group. Most missionaries have the ability to gather a small group of people for the sake of spiritual growth and missional outreach. What most missionaries generally lack, however, is the vision and equipping to do so. Few churches are casting this vision of everyday missionaries gathering people *from* the community *for* community.

Gaining Energy by Gathering

The gathering together of believers for the sake of equipping and mobilization is what God invites and commends to us:

> "And let us consider how we may spur one another on toward love and good deeds, not giving up meeting together, as some are in the habit of doing, but encouraging one another — and all the more as you see the Day approaching" (Hebrews 10:24-25).

These gatherings are like spurs goading believers out of lethargy and laziness and into love in action. Gatherings are like individual logs being placed together to create a bonfire of mission.

John Wesley didn't stop with his Holy Club at Oxford. He went on to spark a revival movement that impacted both England and America in the late 1700s. Wesley's followers were labeled "Methodists" because of the structured nature of the ministry and discipleship methods Wesley used. Wesley prescribed three weekly methods that every believer needed to take a part in if they were serious about revival: societies, class meetings, and bands.

"Societies" were large group gatherings where Christians would come together for the purpose of worshipping and being taught the Scriptures. Out of these societies formed "class meetings" where these same believers would divide up and meet in small groups to discuss how they might help one another truly live out their pursuit of personal holiness and obedience to God. Finally, from these class meetings flowed a series of "bands" where three or four members of the same sex (men with men and women with women) would gather to hold one another accountable.[13]

Many historians have said it was the classes and bands that propelled the movement that gave birth to millions of Christians and thousands of churches. There is dynamic spiritual energy when believers support each other and hold one another accountable for the implementation of the Word of God. Gatherings have significant inherent capacity latent in them.

It's the difference between individual logs that are aflame and logs piled together to create a bonfire. Bonfires create exponentially more light and heat. Like an exponentially growing fire, the flywheel is place of energy creation. As individual disciples come together, their energy from God turns into synergy. Synergy is the benefit that results when two or more agents work together to achieve something they couldn't have achieved on their own. It's the concept of the whole being greater than the sum of its parts. As everyday missionaries creatively start faith-based gatherings and people begin to encourage one another, a synergistic flywheel effect begins to happen.

Three Examples of Starting Faith-Based Gatherings

The mobilization flywheel really starts taking off when believers turn into everyday missionaries. I know three people who serve as great examples of exactly this:

My friend Fernando (whom I mentioned in the previous chapter) felt led to start a lunch-hour Bible study with his three new disciples at the utility company he worked at. Although apprehensive, Fernando went to his boss and asked for permission. His boss was reluctant, but with strict guidelines approved the idea. Fernando started cautiously inviting people in his department to come join him and his three friends. Soon over a dozen church people, new believers and nonbelievers were meeting in the lunch room for a simple time of prayer and Bible study. Lives were being transformed by the Word and Spirit. The group members started asking the Lord how they could better serve those at their work place. All kinds of needs began to be met by those in this small gathering. The kingdom was advancing.

Sam was a rental bus driver at the Phoenix airport for a small rental car company. Sam felt like every group of people who joined him for the approximately twenty-minute ride were his "congregation for the moment." He would play worship music, engage in conversations, offer to pray for people, share short Scriptures. Some of his riders were weekly travelers who became regulars at his "church." Sam was leading a unique faith-based gathering.

Louisa was a pastor's daughter who became disillusioned with church buildings and straight rows of chairs. She loved Jesus and people but was done with "Church, Inc." Louisa began to invite some of her friends to go on Sunday-morning hikes together. They would share some Scripture, sing a song, share their needs, and pray for one another. Then they would hike together for three to four hours. A few people came in relationship with Jesus through the hiking group. This faith-based gathering became a basis of faith development and outreach.

Missionaries must always be looking toward the possibility of catalyzing a gathering of believers. Not all missionaries will have the gifting or skills necessary to initiate and lead "gatherings," but they should all be helping their disciples engage in a small group of believers.

One of the most astute observers of the church in the last four decades is Roberta Hestenes, who wrote, "Small groups have emerged as one of the most potent instruments available to the Christian church for growth, renewal, service, and outreach both in the United States and throughout the world."[14] Forty percent of Americans said they were involved in some kind of small group that met regularly, including twelve-step programs and hobby-based groups. Sixty percent of those groups were related to faith communities.[15]

Yet, as a discipleship and mobilization tool, these small group gatherings are being ignored by most Christians. David Kinnaman from Barna Research says,

> Only 20 percent of Christian adults are involved in some sort of discipleship activity — and this includes a wide range of activities such as attending Sunday school or fellowship group, meeting with a spiritual mentor, studying the Bible with a group, or reading and discussing a Christian book with a group.[16]

Gatherings must be intentionally purposed toward personal spiritual *and* missional growth, or they languish as mere social groups. If "gatherings" are not combined with "goings," the group will fall short of developing each participant's ministry capacity.

Several years ago, Deb and I moved to a new neighborhood believing God had sent us there on assignment. We built relationships with our neighbors and saw God work in amazing ways in individual lives. At one point we felt God was calling us to take it up a notch and start a Bible Study gathering in our house. We dragged our feet but finally capitulated and said, "Yes, Lord."

We were so glad we surrendered! When we began to meet together, something supernatural started to happen. Believers began to grow then go out to serve the neighborhood in new ways. The gathering brought a powerful new dimension of life not only to one another but also to our community.

Then at a funeral — and this happened just recently — I reconnected with a woman from that original group. She had relocated to another city, and we had lost touch. One of the first things she announced to me was, "You would be proud of me. I am leading a group now and wonderful things are happening in the lives of people." I thought to myself, *I had no idea our group was alive in an entirely different city.*

The Variety and Gifts of Gatherings

Gatherings can be as diverse as the individuals who comprise them. This assortment is actually a benefit in effectively reaching out in a cultural context, which has become unimaginably complex. Though diverse, most faith-based gatherings will supply the following advantages:

- A space for people to be encouraged, known, loved, and valued

- A unique setting for all the "one another" passages of Scripture and spiritual gifts to be discovered, developed, and practiced

- A context to evangelize through the hospitality, belonging, and support they offer

- An opportunity for individual disciples to grow into a spiritual family that is "on mission" together

- An environment for individual calling to be discovered

There are a wide variety of kinds of "faith-based gatherings": Discipleship groups, missional communities, mini-church, micro-church, micro-sites, prayer groups, Bible study groups, exploration groups, Alpha groups, book clubs, affinity groups, work place groups, neighborhood gatherings, service groups, spiritual formation groups, recovery groups, fellowship groups, coffee clubs, marketplace groups, cell groups, MOPS groups, Discovery Bible Study groups, etc. Each brand of gathering comes with its strengths and weaknesses.

These groups offer various dimensions of spiritual development that individual evangelism and one-on-one discipleship cannot fully offer, including "body life," "relationship building," "gift empowerment," "leadership training," and increased "missional engagement." The power of gatherings to evangelize through the hospitality, belonging, and life-sharing they offer has been well demonstrated throughout the history of Christianity, starting with the first church.

Acts 2:46-47 implies a link between the fellowship in the home gatherings and the effective evangelism the early Christians practiced. It states,

> Every day they continued to meet together in the temple courts. They broke bread in their homes and ate together with glad and sincere hearts, praising God and enjoying the favor of all the people. And the Lord added to their number daily those who were being saved.

These gatherings also act as incubators to help grow the individual disciples into a spiritual family that is "on mission" together. Depending on what type of group the "gathering" is, it will assign priority ranking to a few or all of these dimensions: 1) fellowship, 2) worship, 3) study/teaching, 4) prayer, 5) service, 6) evangelism, 7) mission, 8) skill development, 9) leadership training, and 10) sending.

The constant temptation and potential downfall of such groups is to become:

- Ingrown, internally focused, and self-serving

- Holy huddles creating comfort zones for non-missional Christians

- A place for escaping the world instead of engaging the world

Consequently, there is a need to keep the groups engaged in missional expressions and multiplication of the gatherings. Different gatherings will have varying trajectories and outcomes. Below you will read of six possible outcomes from the time when a gathering is initiated. None of the following six outcomes is entirely negative. Our intention would be to, at minimum, rise above the first two results. Our desire would be to see all gatherings rise to the final two outcomes.

Six Potential Results of Gatherings:

Misfire — The gathering fails to meet its purpose and disbands. The gathering was well-intentioned but for a variety of reasons, usually lack of healthy leadership, never provides significant spiritual advancement in the lives of the believers.

Maintain — The gathering accomplishes little, except keeping believers together. This group has low expectations, low accountability, and little external focus. The primary purpose for gathering is the social value between members.

Mature — The gathering helps individuals grow spiritually but misses the mobilization piece. These gatherings help people learn and also bring about spiritual transformation, yet lack the missional or multiplication DNA that empowers them to have kingdom impact as a group.

Mission — The gathering prioritizes "gather" then "going," growing spirituality and serving externally. It helps believers grow by assisting them to discover their gifts, strengths, talents, resource, opportunities, and callings. Then the group mobilizes these disciples to serve in those identified giftings, either individually or as part of the group.

These are the two gatherings to which we desire to see all gatherings move:

Multiply — The gathering not only does "mission" but it also sends out leaders (or members) to start other similar groups. This gathering has a high value on reproduction and multiplication of itself. Leadership development is a key characteristic. Shared leadership is the norm as apprentices are recruited, trained, then given leadership roles or are sent to pioneer new gatherings.

Morph — The gathering decides to transition and morph into a new local church. In addition to being on mission and multiplying, this gathering senses a calling from the Spirit to mature and fulfill the biblical requirements to become a distinct church. It transitions from being a ministry of a church to a church doing ministry. (More on the distinction between a gathering and a church in the next two chapters.) This gathering starts a new mobilization flywheel.

Alan Hirsch has emphasized how faith-based gatherings need to move past merely "community," which is bourgeois and safe, to "communitas," which is formed in situations where individuals are driven together because they are being marginalized by the surrounding society.[17] "Community" seeks to create a safe place, but "communitas" calls the group to reach out from the safe place to the margins, to adventure with God into the hurting and even scary places of the city.

Everyday missionaries who create gatherings must remain joyfully aware of the latent energy available *if* the group can move forward into God's calling. As these gatherings form and mature, their potential to be a powerful force for the mobilization of believers and the multiplication of the church grows exponentially!

It is to this ability of a faith-based gathering to birth or build a church that we look next.

CHAPTER 4

The New Churches:
Multiplying Church

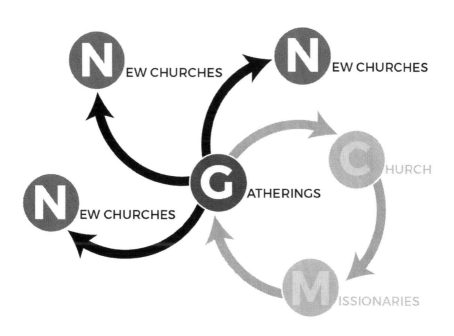

THE NEW CHURCHES

In 1954, a downtown church of about one hundred fifty attendees felt God asking them to start a new church in an area of town that was starting to boom. So the pastor asked a few members who lived in that new area to start praying about reaching their neighbors. They began praying and witnessing with a new fervor and soon a few folks had been won to Christ. Rather than bringing them seven miles away to the downtown church, the pastor said, "Let's start a Bible study in your neighborhood and one of you can lead it." That's exactly what happened, and it began to grow. Soon the group was asking the pastor if they could become a new church.

With the blessing and encouragement of the downtown church, the gathering of disciples organized themselves into a new church called Light & Life. Thirty-seven years later, Deb and I walked onto the platform and were installed as the pastors of Light & Life. Now twenty-eight years have flowed by and Light & Life has launched multiple churches by doing for others what was done for us long before we arrived.

God calls disciples, gatherings, and churches to multiply:

> So the church throughout all Judea and Galilee and Samaria had peace and was being built up. And walking in the fear of the Lord and in the comfort of the Holy Spirit, it multiplied. (Acts 9:31, ESV)

This passage is an overarching summary statement of a myriad of missional and discipleship activities and faith-based gatherings that were happening throughout Judea, Galilee, and Samaria. While we are not privy to exact details of what was happening, we may confidently assume disciples were reaching nonbelievers, creating gatherings of believers, and many of these were becoming established churches. This resulted in the multiplication of the church as a whole.

The "end game" of the gathering is not longevity but productivity, especially through mobilization and multiplication. The mother church that birthed our church has not existed for 30 years, yet her "once upon a time" faith and courage continue to produce children, grandchildren, and great-grandchildren.

Building the Mobilization Flywheel:
100% of churches can become mobilization stations that equip and send believers.
100% of believers have the calling and ability to be everyday missionaries where they live, work, or play.
100% of everyday missionaries can play a role in gatherings.
Most everyday missionaries can form and lead a gathering of seekers or believers.
Many gatherings can become new churches led by everyday missionaries (who are predominately bi-vocational).

We love small groups of believers coming together for fellowship. We do think, however, most groups are shortsighted. They are often an extension of a self-serving mindset where believers are primarily asking, "What's in it for me?" Too few groups have a kingdom mindset, believing they are coming together for the sake of kingdom expansion. Once a gathering catches hold of the mobilization mindset, they start asking different questions, dreaming different dreams, and seeking different goals.

Three Ways Healthy Gatherings Expand the Kingdom:

1. Gatherings Strengthen Existing Churches

   All gatherings should strengthen the health of the "sending" church. As gatherings bring together people from the mission fields, these disciples can be connected with the existing "sending" church. These strengthened believers, who now have a missional and mobilized mindset, can become active and immensely productive in the overall life of an existing local church.

   A biblical example: Perhaps Apollos had an experience similar to what is described above. We know that when Apollos came to Ephesus he was preaching in the synagogue what he knew. But he was unattached and uninitiated to the church of Jesus. Priscilla and Aquila invited him to the gathering that met in their home. There Priscilla and Aquila (and undoubtedly the brothers and sisters, as seen in Acts 18:27) schooled Apollos in the person, work, and ways of Jesus. The believers spoke faith and encouragement into his life. They recognized his giftedness and blessed it. When Apollos was ready, the Ephesian believers were openhanded with their new brother and sent him to the church at Achaia to strengthen it.

In the gathering Deb and I started in our house (see Chapter 3) there were two couples who attended the mother church about 20 minutes away. As these couples participated in a neighborhood group that was living on mission, they became zealous advocates in our mother church for this type of mobilization. There were three other people in our gathering who were nominal Christians when they came into our group. They occasionally attended a small, lifeless church in an adjacent neighborhood. When our gathering decided to become a church, rather than jumping in with our new church plant, they went back into their church with a new zeal and an effective impact. The result was that the particular local church and the kingdom were expanded.

2. Gatherings Reproduce Themselves

All gatherings have the ability to mobilize everyday missionaries into their unique personal mission fields. Many of these missionaries have the ability to repeat the cycle and launch new faith-based gatherings out of the existing gatherings. This multiplication of groups becomes an effective expansion of the kingdom.

A biblical example: In Acts 6:1-7 we find the number of disciples in Jerusalem increasing. We know from Acts 2:46 that these disciples were meeting in homes. It is also clear from Acts 6:3 that new leaders were being recognized. It is probable, then, that the seven men who were selected to give broader based ministry were already carrying out leadership in the home gatherings that were happening. To accommodate the growing number of disciples mentioned in Acts 6:1 and 6:7 it is almost certain the home gatherings were multiplying. New leaders were being raised up and sent to start new gatherings, which together comprised the church at Jerusalem.

A modern-day example is Fernando's noon Bible study group at the utility company (mentioned above). Some of the members began to reach out in their own departments and before long these "missionaries" were starting their own Bible studies at lunchtime. The gospel was multiplying and advancing.

Sometimes this multiplication of the gathering will be in the form of raising up a new leader and sending them out to start an actual church. Rather than the gathering becoming a new church itself, the gathering remains intact while giving birth to a new church by sending a leader.

As the gathering matures, the gifts of the various members are discovered, developed, and given expression. Often there will be one or more who have apostolic giftings. The gathering then has to decide how to affirm and deploy the gifts of the apostle. Depending on the maturity and calling of the person, the group may commission the apostolic missionary to purposefully go to start a new gathering that will become a church.

3. Gatherings Become New Churches

Some gatherings carry the DNA of healthy churches and have the potential, with intentionality, to mature into new churches. These "missionary to gathering to church" lifecycles are especially important because they organically carry the fullness of Jesus into the various domains of society and are born with a solid disciple-making and mobilization culture.

As faith-based gatherings develop, they often desire to evolve into a church. As people are added, relationships are built, gifts are shared, Scriptures are taught, prophecies are given, leaders develop, a shepherd or shepherds are raised up, and as the vision of what could happen for the kingdom becomes clearer, *then* there is often a progression from a gathering to a church. (Exactly when that shift happens is the subject of Chapter 5 and Chapter 6).

A biblical example: In Philippi, Lydia was leading a prayer meeting at the river, probably a regular gathering of God-fearers (Acts 16:13-15). When Paul arrived, he proclaimed the gospel of Jesus to hearts that were wide open to the true God. A joyful baptism happened, followed by a "party" at Lydia's over-sized house. This gathering of believers at Lydia's place would soon be joined by a local "jailer" and his entire family (Acts 16:30-34). It is probable, but not certain, that Lydia's house remained a central gathering place for the believers in Philippi.

At some point the "gathering at Philippi" became the "church of Philippi." We know that approximately 10 years later Paul would write in Philippians 1:1, "Paul and Timothy, servants of Christ Jesus, To all God's holy people in Christ Jesus at Philippi …." This gathering had matured into a fully functioning church. The mobilization flywheel was at work!

Lydia may have been "an everyday missionary" reaching people for the true God through her daily business life. We do know she had brought her network (Acts 16:15, *oikos*) to the river for prayer on the Sabbath. She seems to have led her household in being baptized. Lydia persuaded Paul, Timothy, and their missionary companions to lodge with them for a time (Acts 16:15, 40). The discipleship of Lydia and others was undoubtedly taking place during that stay. The gathering of believers at Philippi grew and matured, eventually adding elders and deacons and becoming a new church. Then workers and gospel servants, like Epaphroditus, were sent out (Phil. 2:25).

Lydia's story reminds me of Wade Burnett. Wade is a brilliant and nationally recognized lawyer who has argued cases in front of the United States Supreme Court. His work has been featured in *The New York Times* and *People* magazine and on ABC's *20/20*, NBC's *Dateline*, *Good Morning America*, and through many other media outlets. In Wade's law practice in Louisiana, he developed a spiritual burden for his co-workers in the law firm. Wade then started a Bible study in the conference room of the firm. People began to have their lives changed by the power of the gospel and the wisdom of the Word of God. They invited more friends, and soon the conference room was bursting at the seams. Wade, the lawyer and the everyday missionary, was also becoming Wade, the pastor.

As the gathering shared life together, it became apparent to the group and to Wade that this was not just an overgrown small group; rather it was the seed of a new church. Soon Wade led the group to become a church. It wasn't long until the church left the conference room and became a powerful ministry in the broader community.

The Great Potential of Faith-Based Gatherings

The gathering Deb and I started in our house (mentioned in Chapter 3) grew and multiplied into another group. Another one of our leaders living in the area started another group. Our vision grew with the group. Soon we felt called to more, called to launch a Sunday-evening church. From these three groups, a healthy church impacting a very lost, churchless community was started. This church would go on to send multiple missionaries and ministers to the harvest field.

After Jesus' resurrection, his small group of twelve continued to meet together for prayer, Scripture reading, worship, and breaking bread. This small group gathered others. On the day of Pentecost, this gathering hit a divine "inflection point" transitioning into the first church. In Acts 1, they were a prayer meeting, but by the end of Acts 2, they were a church.

Faith-based groups have tremendous potential to birth new churches and to produce kingdom expansion.

Healthy faith-based gatherings need to ask God what he would have for their future. Many of the gatherings have "new church" potential in them. To tap into that potential requires discernment, vision, faith, and sacrifice. The actual step of becoming a church is largely dependent upon factors considered in the next two chapters.

Questions to Consider

- Can neighborhood gatherings reach people the local church cannot?

- Can mobilization gatherings "infect" their church with a new passion for discipleship and mission?

- Are gatherings ideal places for raising up new leaders for kingdom work?

- Can gatherings reproduce themselves by launching new groups?

- Can gatherings raise up apostolic members to send out to start new churches?

- Can gatherings equip disciples to be significant participants in church planting teams?

- Can gatherings mature into autonomous churches?

CHAPTER 5

The Friction Points: Setting the Ministry Standards

One of the "enemies" of the mobilization flywheel is "friction points." With regard to the flywheel, engineers have worked diligently to reduce it. They are seeking to remove any resistance that will slow down the flywheel. For example, to prevent friction, they've dispensed of using physical bearings. Instead they use "magnetic bearings" that levitate the spinning wheel and permanently suspend it in place.[18] These bearings are continuously lifting up the flywheel to keep it as free of friction as possible. They help the flywheel spin.

In the mobilization flywheel, there are different friction-producing "drags" which can slow or even stop the flywheel from spinning. At the same time, however, there are certain standards of "bearings" that are necessary for the flywheel to be attached, balanced, and effective.

In this chapter, we will look at the adjustments of some of those bearings so as to create as little drag on the mission as possible while keeping the mission healthily aligned.

Glory and Fruit, Surrender and Service

Two passages serve as key instructions for mobilization:

> John 15:8: "This is to my Father's glory, that you bear much fruit, showing yourselves to be my disciples."

> Matthew 6:9-10: "This, then, is how you should pray: 'Our Father in heaven, hallowed be your name, your kingdom come, your will be done, on earth as it is in heaven.'"

The verse in John is about glory and fruit. We are called to bear much fruit, not simply to be faithful. The verses in Matthew are about surrender and service — our will submitted to God's will to partner in seeing God's kingdom come to earth.

The logic goes something like this:

If the chief end of humans is to bring God glory,

And if a primary means of bringing God glory is to maximize our fruitfulness (fruitfulness being a key demonstration of our discipleship according to John 15:8),

→ Then our motivation for results in ministry must be seeing our Father's name revered and exalted (Matt. 6:9-10).

Our objective must be the expansion of his kingdom without concern for our own kingdom. The Lord's Prayer reveals that the daily surrender of our will to his will is an essential key to kingdom-building.

These truths must form the foundation for mobilization of believers through our churches. Otherwise, we will seek to collect saints *around* us rather than send missionaries *from* us.

We will create *obstacles* instead of *opportunities* for people fulfilling their full destiny.

This understanding becomes essential as we begin to determine our criteria for the different stages on the mobilization flywheel.

> **Building the Mobilization Flywheel:**
>
> *100% of churches can become mobilization stations that equip and send believers.*
>
> *100% of believers have the calling and ability to be everyday missionaries where they live, work, or play.*
>
> *100% of everyday missionaries can play a role in gatherings.*
>
> *Most everyday missionaries can form and lead a gathering of seekers or believers.*
>
> *Many gatherings can become new churches led by everyday missionaries (who are predominately bi-vocational).*
>
> **This mobilization process is helped or hindered by the criteria set by your church, denomination, or tribe.**

Drags and Aids

Between each point of the mobilization flywheel are drags or aids: Drags create friction, thus slowing or stopping the flywheel. Aids reduce friction, thus increasing the speed of the flywheel.

Church doctrines, culture, governance structures, policies, and leadership criteria create drags or aids for the mobilization of the body of Christ. Most church leaders knowingly (or unknowingly) build drags that prohibit mobilization. Few leaders are excellent at removing friction points and aiding mobilization for the kingdom.

These friction points (drags) or friction reduction agents (aids) do not exist on an either/or basis but on a continuum of various aspects. Some of the continuum dynamics are:

Drags	Aids
Institutional ecclesiology	Movement ecclesiology
Complexity	Simplicity
Attendance metrics	Discipleship metrics
Clergy-centric structures	Priesthood of all believers
Celebrity pastors	Hero-makers
Theological emphasis	Ministry-equippers
Curriculum discipleship	Relational discipleship
Neglect of individual gifts	Gift empowerment
Resistance	Encouragement
Unbelief	Faith
Territoriality	Kingdom-mindedness
Insecurity	Security
Self-focused individuals	Mission-focused individuals
Mistrust	Ample trust
Rigidity	Adaptability
Apathy	Passion
Ignorance	Knowledge
Empty tradition	Innovation
Maintenance of status quo	Vision
Isolation	Networking
Solo focus	Team focus

These are just some of the cultural points which serve as friction spots for each point on the mobilization flywheel.

Seven Principles of Mobilization from Ancient Antioch

The church of ancient Antioch is undoubtedly the clearest example of a friction-reducing church in the New Testament. We can learn much from the kind of aid their church provide. In Acts 13:1-3, we read about the Antioch church:

> Now in the church at Antioch there were prophets and teachers: Barnabas, Simeon called Niger, Lucius of Cyrene, Manaen (who had been brought up with Herod the tetrarch) and Saul. While they were worshiping the Lord and fasting, the Holy Spirit said, "Set apart for me Barnabas and Saul for the work to which I have called them." *So, after they had fasted and prayed, they placed their hands on them and sent them off.*

From this passage, we can see seven principles from the church at ancient Antioch which impact mobilization:

First, **diversity** — Antioch was being led, taught, inspired, and blessed by a multiplicity of gifted individuals (Barnabas, Simeon, Lucius, Manaen, Saul, and undoubtedly others). Their church culture was not dominated by one super-star leader everyone sat under and listened to. A diversity of gifts in a variety of leaders created an atmosphere conducive to raising others up into their destiny.

As a ministry leader, ask yourself: *Am I giving an adequate platform to a diversity of voices and gifts? Am I expecting effective ministers to sound like our key leader sounds?*

Second, **faithfulness** — Barnabas and Saul were actively serving in their local church and community. They were faithfully fulfilling what they knew to do for the kingdom. Remember, Abraham only received guidance when he started moving in faith, not knowing where he might end up. As the old adage admonishes, "It's hard to steer a parked car."

As a ministry leader, ask yourself: *Am I activating our people into service where they are right now? Do I teach believers to be faithful with their "now" instead of waiting for their "then"?*

Third, **discernment** — Barnabas and Saul were actively listening for the Spirit's guidance and further calling "for the work to which I have called them" (Acts 13:2, ESV). While being faithful where they were, they were open for the "more" God might have for them. Consequently, they heard the Spirit's new and expanded call.

As a ministry leader, ask yourself: *Do I help believers dream about their "more" or try to limit their vision to inside our church's ministry?*

Fourth, **kingdom priority** — the Antioch church was kingdom-minded and open-handed. Antioch had a sizeable mission to reach their city for Christ. Their greater mission, however, was to extend the kingdom of God as effectively and widely as possible. They were asking God how to reach beyond their own context.

As a ministry leader, ask yourself: *Is our church more concerned with local church success than overall kingdom fruitfulness? Does a missionary or church plant have to have our brand or name on them before we empower and send them?*

Fifth, **affirmation** — the Antioch church worshipped, prayed, and fasted for guidance on how to reach the greater harvest, how to minister the gospel more effectively, whom to send out on a special apostolic mission. Barnabas and Saul's inward, personal calls were affirmed by their local church out of a time of seeking the Spirit's direction for mission.

As a ministry leader, ask yourself: *Is our church marked by prayer and fasting for the mission? Do we expect the Spirit to give revelation, instruction, and guidance to empower believers into their full destiny?*

Sixth, **empowerment** — the Antioch church entered into another season of fasting and prayer. (Bear in mind, fasting doesn't happen in a one-hour prayer meeting.) This second time of prayer was directed not toward discernment but empowerment. The church knew they were sending a dynamic duo out on a mission that would be dangerous and beyond their own strength to accomplish. Therefore, the church fasted and prayed to be able to send them out in the power of the Spirit. Much of the fruitfulness of the mission would flow not just from Barnabas and Saul's giftings but also from the power of those praying for them.

As a ministry leader, ask yourself: *How essential to me are seasons of prayer for the purpose of empowering believers in their callings? Do I teach believers to form teams of prayer partners to cover them in their gospel work?*

Seventh, **commissioning** — the Antioch church commissioned Barnabas and Saul by the laying on of hands. In Scripture, the laying on of hands usually conveys one of these four realities: a blessing being imparted, the filling of the Holy Spirit, the impartation of a gift of the Spirit, or the placing of a believer into church leadership. It is possible to see an aspect of all four of these at work here in this passage.

Primarily this commissioning was a public, church-wide dedication and official launching of the mission to which God had called Barnabas and Saul. It was also a goodbye party since there was a distinct possibility they may not ever return. It is reasonable to believe Saul and Barnabas often reflected on this commissioning by the Antioch church. They, undoubtedly, drew strength from this cherished memory and from the promises of ongoing prayer that were heard there.

As a ministry leader, ask yourself: *What markers do I have to signify people are embracing their next stage of ministry deployment? What symbolic acts do I practice to commission people into their next phase of ministry? How well do I celebrate the mission-callings of our people?*

We believe the Antioch process should be an instructional model for churches as they empower missionaries, gatherings, and new churches. Antioch forms a backdrop for churches thinking through their standards and approach to the three major transfer points of the mobilization flywheel.

Transfer Points of the Mobilization Flywheel

The transfer points are the places where the flywheel progresses through its revolution. In our mobilization application, they are the places where new realities of the mission emerge.

We find the early church's criteria for everyday missionaries in 1 Peter 2:9: "But you are a chosen people, a royal priesthood, a holy nation, God's special possession, that you may declare the praises of him who called you out of darkness into his wonderful light." Each local church, denomination, or network must establish their doctrine and practice of "the priesthood of all believers."

It's appropriate to ask:

1. How far did Peter mean for us to take this "royal priesthood" (1 Peter 2:9)?

2. To what extent is the ordinary, individual believer entrusted and empowered to carry out the ministry of the gospel?

3. Who is trusted to "make disciples"?

4. What "holy" functions may a typical everyday missionary administer with the blessing of the church?

On one end of the continuum is a very formal, structured view of the roles of ministers. This may include much preparation, education, and training before the everyday missionary is entrusted with the discipleship of another person.

On the other end of the continuum is an informal, organic approach to ministry. This may include little to no preparation for the everyday missionary. This might be a "hand a believer a Bible and tell them to go start reading it with someone who doesn't know Jesus" approach.

This continuum would also include a spectrum to identify who is authorized to perform sacerdotal duties, those "priestly" functions more commonly reserved for formal church leadership.

Questions to Consider

- Who can serve communion in a church service? Where can communion be served?

- Who can baptize a new believer? Where can baptism be performed?

- Is baptism only to be done in a formal church setting with a group of witnesses by an elder of the church? Or does a pond beside the road function just as well (Acts 8:36)?

- Who can perform marriages? What prerequisites (aside from legal considerations) must a "royal priest" meet to exercise authority to join two as one?

- Who can bury people? Can the ordinary Jesus-follower in your church perform funerals?

Local churches, often directed by their denominations, must assess and communicate the answer to these kinds of questions.

The church's criteria for gatherings: As church leadership seeks to reduce the "drag" and increase the "aid" in helping gatherings multiply, there are appropriate questions that need to be asked. There are two key Scriptures to be considered and applied for the flywheel to keep its bearings:

James 3:1: "Not many of you should become teachers, my fellow believers, because you know that we who teach will be judged more strictly."

2 Timothy 2:2: "And the things you have heard me say in the presence of many witnesses entrust to reliable people who will also be qualified to teach others."

James warns us about the stricter judgment for those whom are empowered or are self-appointed as teachers. Paul admonishes Timothy to only hand off the teaching duties to "reliable people who will also be qualified to teach others." There seems to be some criteria for those who teach at Christian gatherings.

For a gathering to stay in balance and avoid wobbling toward unhealthiness, consider three areas of thought:

The leadership of the gathering. Each church must set their standards for who can initiate, lead, and teach a gathering, small group, or missional community. Again, there is a wide continuum of thought and practice on this subject. On the highly structured, more formal end of the continuum, some churches reject small groups outside of the church for fear of biblical teaching being distorted. Only trained theologians and teachers can be trusted to teach the Bible to other believers.

Other churches champion small groups as long as the following are in place: an extensive training course is completed, they are apprenticed into the role, the curriculum is strictly controlled, and there is ongoing and high accountability for the leaders.

On the other end of the continuum are the churches where any believer with a Bible can gather friends and family to meet together for spiritual or missional purposes (or both). These gatherings can be organized with no endorsement, no prerequisite training, and no formal accountability from the local church.

The content of the gathering. Another part of this continuum is what is allowed or encouraged within the life of the group. Some churches allow only regimented, curriculum-driven content and prayer. Even personal life-sharing may be discouraged lest a form of nonprofessional and unsanctioned "counseling" transpire.

On the other end of the spectrum are churches who entrust small group leaders to act as "mini-pastors" to their group. Communion, baptisms, child dedications, offerings, and even weddings can happen within the context of the group's life.

Some churches have ongoing accountability and resourcing structures maintaining high levels of control for quality assurances for each of the groups. Others have little or no requirements or oversight for their groups, believing the Word and Spirit to be adequate. Some churches reason: *Well, Paul started groups then shortly left them with uneducated leaders with almost no means of continuing his oversight, except an occasional letter, and that worked out fairly well.*

The mission of the gathering. Expectations for the mission of the gatherings must be determined as well. For some groups the goal is simply fellowship, for others it is highly evangelistic or for the study of the Bible or missional service in the community. Some groups are to be closed, some are to reach out and grow but not multiply. For others, multiplication is the primary goal.

The selected goals impact the expected duration of the group. Some groups are established for a definitive period of time such as a season or a semester. But the intention for other gatherings is that they take on an enduring life of their own. (My in-laws, for example, were in the same small group for 30 years.)

Questions to Consider

- Who can convene such a gathering?

- What preparation or training must a leader complete before being empowered to start groups?

- What ongoing expectations will be placed on the leader by the local church?

- What level of accountability does the group leader have to the leaders of the church?

- What ongoing attachment does the gathering have to the local church?

- What role can the convener/leader fill? What latitudes do they have?

- Must they use a defined curriculum or can lessons streamed from a website be used?

- What kind of activities, especially spiritual activities, can the group initiate and conduct?

- What kind of expectations or freedoms does the group have to multiply?

A Church's Criteria for New Churches

Each local church or church "tribe" must determine how they will define "church." Establishing the criteria for identifying when a gathering might transition into an entity accurately titled "church" is vital. Two of the Scriptures which speak to this are:

> Titus 1:5: "The reason I left you in Crete was that you might put in order what was left unfinished and appoint elders in every town, as I directed you."

> Acts 14:23: "Paul and Barnabas appointed elders for them in each church and, with prayer and fasting, committed them to the Lord, in whom they had put their trust."

There is a distinction between a gathering and a "church": gatherings have at least one characteristic of a healthy church but not all. A church has all essential functions or characteristics which meet or exceed one's defined ecclesiology.

To use Titus 1:5-language, this decision must be determined when a church has been "put in order" and not "left unfinished." Titus 1:5 and Acts 14:23 emphasize the appointment of elders indicating some level of leadership, structure, authority, and accountability. Establishing the criteria for identifying when a "gathering" becomes a biblical "church" is of critical importance. Jesus intends that every believer needs and deserves a biblically true church family.

By making this decision two risks threaten our gatherings: setting the bar too high and setting the bar too low for the church:

- *If you set the bar too low,* you will rob people of the full power of biblical family. The gathering will be something less than what the New Testament defines as church.

- *If you set the bar too high,* you will stifle the mobilization of everyday missionaries and limit the multiplication of new churches. The believers will experience institutional church with layers of human-produced traditions. It will be something different than what the New Testament describes as church.

In either scenario, the believer is left with something other than the healthy biblical church God intended for his people to enjoy and benefit from.

While it is true that every believer is a *representative* of the "universal church" and every gathering of believers is an *expression* of the "universal church," it does not follow that every ongoing gathering is in itself a "local church." Scripture indicates there are certain characteristics which must be true of a gathering before it qualifies as a "church."

If the word "church" is used to describe any and every group of Christians gathered together, it robs believers of the healthy, biblical community God ordained for them. It sends an erroneous message to the world as they watch for the spiritual family Jesus offers them.

At this point, recall the three examples we gave in Chapter 3 and ask yourself:

1. Is Sam's gathering on the rental car shuttle bus actually a "church"?

2. Has Louisa's hiking group become a real "church" for her?

3. Is Fernando's current lunchtime Bible study a bona fide "church" for those who attend?

Answers to questions like these depend on where the bar is set for your definition of "church."

A Low-Bar Definition

On the positive side, an overly minimal definition of "church" may open the door for more missionaries to plant churches and for the rapid multiplication of churches, thus producing a higher quantity of "churches."

On the negative side, an overly minimal or sloppy definition of "church" may open a door for:

- A self-centered, self-affirming, self-regulating version of Christianity and community

- Error (or even heresy) in doctrine or lifestyle

- A temporality to the "church" which leaves it with a less-enduring impact upon the community

- A hobbling of believers growing to their full maturity in Christ

- A hindering to believers enjoying a healthier expression of the body of Christ

A High-Bar Definition

On the positive side, an overly complicated, restrictive definition of "church" may result in a purer form of doctrinal understanding and sacred practices. Increased reverence for sacraments means grape soda and Doritos don't cut it for communion. It can produce a higher quality of churches.

On the negative side, an excessively complicated, restrictive definition of "church" may open a door for:

- A legalistic, pharisaical version of Christianity and community

- A nearly nonreproducible model of church which slows or stops the expansion of the church

- An overly exclusive group of leaders

- An over-controlling authority structure hobbling missional and creative expressions

- A hampering of believers in growing into maturity (often due to an exaggerated "leadership reliance")

- A hindering to believers moving into their calling and the fullness of their destiny

Questions to Consider

- What doctrines must be present?

- What functions must be practiced?

- What mission must be pursued?

- What leaders must be in position?

- How are leaders placed in position?

- What defines membership/partnership/belonging?

- What accountability exists between members? Between leaders and members?

- What discipline ensures group morality?

Each church or tribe of churches will need to give prayerful and thoughtful attention to setting the standards. Leaders will need to make these decisions with a bias toward the mission of the gospel saturation and simultaneously with a high respect for the sacredness of the church. These decisions will necessarily stem from a well-defined, essential biblical ecclesiology. To this we now turn.

CHAPTER 6

The Ecclesiology: Defining the Essentials of Church

YOUR MINIMUM ECCLESIOLOGY

THE ECCLESIOLOGY

When is the name "church" a true description of a gathering?

Shakespeare said, "A rose by another other name would smell as sweet."[19] A church by any other name would still have the beauty and fragrance of a church. But if you mislabel a fragrance-free dahlia a "rose," you will miss the fragrance only a real rose can deliver. When we write on "minimal ecclesiology," we are primarily focusing on the essential attributes of a gathering that qualify it to be accurately titled "church." We're talking about a local church like the church of Corinth: "To the church of God in Corinth, to those sanctified in Christ Jesus and called to be His holy people, together with all those everywhere who call on the name of our Lord Jesus Christ — their Lord and ours" (1 Cor. 1:2).

Building the Mobilization Flywheel:
100% of churches can become mobilization stations that equip and send believers.
100% of believers have the calling and ability to be everyday missionaries where they live, work, or play.
100% of everyday missionaries can play a role in gatherings.
Most everyday missionaries can form and lead a gathering of seekers or believers.
Many gatherings can become new churches led by everyday missionaries (who are predominately bi-vocational).
This mobilization process is helped or hindered by the criteria set by your church, denomination, or tribe.
100% of these new churches can be "biblically defined churches."

Is This "Church"?

Try asking one hundred pastors to define church and you will get nearly one hundred different answers. Their answers will probably have many similarities. Some will go to the original languages. Others will reach for the Church Fathers. Still others will explain the pragmatic realities that shape what they call church.

As our American culture shifts, as our technologies empower new communication forms, as our population grows even denser in urban areas, as innovative forms of church emerge, new questions are being asked about what comprises "church."

- Is the house church — with its sharing of life and Word and sacraments but with no identified leader or accountability for participants — truly a church?

- Is the highly organized, liturgical church — with its steeple, gilded pulpit, and formal communion but with no true fellowship, no discipleship, or missional expressions — a biblical church?

- Is the fictional "ichurchforyou.org" — with its online gatherings and chat rooms but no physical gathering — a biblical church?

- Is the group that meets Saturday mornings to pray, study Scripture, and pass out food to the homeless but with no baptism, communion, or elders a real church?

- Is the group that goes biking on Sunday mornings after sharing a few verses and prayer an adequate expression of a church?

- Is a gathering a church because we choose to call it by the name "church"?

- Is there a biblical definition for when the term "church" can be accurately used?

God chose not to put a dictionary definition of "church" in our Bibles. There is no chapter which gives a sacred list of what constitutes a real church. The exact definition is left somewhat open-ended.

While God has not written a *prescription* we must follow, there is a *description* we must recognize and honor lest we invent our own definitions of church.

God's descriptions are to help us build authentic, healthy churches without substituting our microwaved recipes or culture-shaped creations and calling it "church."

Three Questions for Church Planters and Church Leaders

1. Does every believer need or deserve a God-honoring, biblically true church?

When we understand the church as a spiritual family God provides for every believer, a related question may be: Does every person deserve a natural family? Absolutely. Why? Because God set up the plan of a natural family and desires for each child to enjoy one. Unfortunately, some children may have to live as orphans. Unlike a natural family, God's spiritual family is available to every child of God. He desires that none of his children live as spiritual orphans.

2. What happens if we think or say we are offering true church but we really are not?

If we are *not* providing a biblically defined spiritual family (an essential church), then we are not giving to our disciples/followers/group members all God desires for them. We are causing them to stop short of God's best. In addition, if we are calling a gathering "church" when it is not, we are misleading people. We are mistaken and inadvertently deceiving others.

In the New Testament, we discover God's portrait of the original and authentic church. In church planting, we are called to reproduce the original thing, not our personal idea of the original.

We must ask, "What are we reproducing?" For example, a copy machine copies what is already there. It doesn't decide to add or subtract elements of the picture while it is reproducing the next copy. We have to be sure we are reproducing something God-honoring and biblical. We must be reproducing and multiplying the original, biblical church.

3. How do we know we are offering the original?

You might ask yourself, *How can we be sure we are striking the balance between what is "less than" church and what is "more than" church?*

Our first house was 60 years old with ugly linoleum floors. We suspected there were solid wood floors underneath, and sure enough after pulling up the linoleum, we started to discover just that. First, though, we found three different layers of various-colored paint. We kept discovering and reached the original floors, and they were beautiful. Through the decades these floors had become lost under the various decorating ideas. Too often, this is a description of churches.

Movements start off with a very simple, natural, beautiful form of church. However, it is natural for humans to begin adding unnecessary elements on top of the original. This usually creates institutions that produce some level of exclusivism. Denominations, networks, academies, and institutions are prone to this. To work against this tendency, "church" must not be "over-defined" with layers of human requirements painted onto the original. So how do we peel away the layers to get to the real thing?

Others tend to oversimplify to the point of redefinition. As we began to redo the wood floors in our first house, we got carried away and sanded too far at certain places. In an effort to resurrect the original beauty, we sacrificed too much of the wood planks. Those spots were no longer useable and we had to replace them.

In the case of oversimplifying the church, too many elements are stripped away until less than the essentials remain. This "simple church" form sometimes ignores a variety of Scriptures while prioritizing others, until nearly every "gathering" of believers is defined as "church."

To reiterate, we find the balance by a careful study of Scripture that leads to a clearly articulated ecclesiology.

Why Does Ecclesiology Matter?

Simply stated, to use the words of Scripture, God has chosen the church to make known his manifold wisdom (see Eph. 3:10). The vehicle of God's choosing to "make known his wisdom" to reach the world is the church; therefore, the "church" is what we must build. The church is the instrument for God's agenda in the world. Therefore, healthy ecclesiology matters because:

1. A group calling themselves a church that is not a church is being deceived and deceiving others.

2. Jesus said *he* would build his church, and if we are building something that is not "church," *we* are building it instead of Jesus building it (Matthew 16:18).

3. Jesus promised to keep reproducing his church. If we aren't "church," we will miss his promise to reproduce us.

4. We desire to multiply what the Bible identifies as "church" and not a substitute or inferior reality.

5. We rob people of the need they have for a fully functioning church family. We stunt their growth and the growth of the kingdom.

6. Without a clear definition, we are not sure what we are aiming for, what we are seeking to build. The clearer the vision, the stronger the mission.

If we set the bar too *low* and oversimplify church, leaving out essential elements that define a biblical church, then:

- We are more susceptible to heresy infiltrating the church and spreading.

- We more easily empower unhealthy or unprepared leaders who will hurt the gospel, believers, and the reputation of the church.

- We more easily empower systems with little or no accountability.

- We begin to "dumb down" the healthy theology of the Scriptures.

- We rob believers of the full and biblical experience of the organized church.

- We wrongly define the church.

Often times "churches" with the bar too low have overemphasized "grace" and underemphasized "truth." They miss the true church.

If we set the bar too *high* and overcomplicate church, adding nonessential or manmade elements to define the church, then:

- We rob believers of the essence and biblical experience of the simple church.

- We make reproduction, and especially multiplication, much more difficult, if not impossible.

- We dramatically shrink the pool of potential church planters.

- We move from an atmosphere of grace to one of legalism.

- We create high-control structures that tend toward institutionalism and away from movement.

- We decrease the number of gatherings that can become churches.

Often times "churches" with the bar too high have overemphasized "truth" and underemphasized "grace." They miss the true church.

Two Key Scriptures on God's Description of the Church

In a discussion of "minimal ecclesiology," it is important to distinguish between the local church and the universal church. The apostle Paul underlines that distinction in 1 Corinthians 1:2:

To the church of God in Corinth, to those sanctified in Christ Jesus and called to be his holy people, together with all those everywhere who call on the name of our Lord Jesus Christ — their Lord and ours.

Paul defines the church here as being those who:

- Have been "sanctified in Christ Jesus"

- Are answering the "call to be his holy people"

- "Call on the name of our Lord Jesus"

- Are in a *specific* place — "the church of God in Corinth"

- Are in *every* place "those everywhere who call on the name of the Lord Jesus Christ"

Paul brings these two expressions of the church side-by-side in this opening to the first Corinthian letter:

" ... together with all those everywhere who call on the name of our Lord Jesus Christ ... "

The term "church" describes *everyone, everywhere* who is in relationship with the head of the body, Jesus. This is what is known as the universal church. This church has no leaders except the head of the church, Jesus the Chief Shepherd.

" ... to the church of God in Corinth ... "

The term "church" describes *certain people,* in *specific places* who are in relationship with the head, Jesus, but also in relationship with particular brothers and sisters. This is the local church. The local church has recognized leadership who work as "under-shepherds" for the Chief Shepherd.

These two manifestations of the church are distinct yet overlapping. All those in the local church of Corinth are also in the universal church, but not all those in the universal church are in the local church of Corinth. It is like saying, "All my Facebook friends are members of Facebook, but not all Facebook members are my Facebook friends."

The second Scripture that is especially helpful in describing the church is Acts 20:28: "Keep watch over yourselves and all the flock of which the Holy Spirit has made you overseers. Be shepherds of the church of God, which he bought with his own blood."

In this passage, Luke describes the church as:

- Those belonging to God — "the church of God"

- Those purchased by the blood of Jesus — "bought with his own blood"

- Those under the guardianship of shepherds — "keep watch over ... all the flock"

- Those under the care of shepherds — "be shepherds of the church"

- Those in a certain place under the guidance of certain leaders — "*the* flock of which the Holy Spirit has made you overseers"

Luke describes a certain flock (i.e., a local church) overseen by under-shepherds. There is an authority of leadership for the sake of the flock described here.

Note what these two Scriptures *don't* say: that it's a certain size, meeting in a defined place, meeting on a specific day, following a prescribed liturgy, demanding a seminarian leader, or even (gasp) taking an offering.

Instead, the church is a flock, a family, a people called together for God's purposes for teaching, protection, guidance, and care by godly leaders.

While there are other descriptions of the church in the New Testament, these two Scriptures are indicative of the fact that God has given some definition while leaving much room for creativity. This means we must work out our own clear definition derived from our understanding of God's Word on the subject. If we are going to go plant "churches," we need to know what we mean when we say "church."

I am privileged to serve as Director of Equipping and Spiritual Engagement for Exponential, and our passion is to see the multiplication of healthy, biblical churches. Exponential embraces a variety of sizes, shapes, forms, and expressions of "church." Depending on your tribe, denomination, network, or personal background, your view of "church" will be shaped toward a simpler or more formal definition.

Exponential does, however, want to assist in clarifying essential ecclesiology in order to empower discipleship, increase the multiplication of the church and help leaders embrace new forms of the church, all while continuing in biblical and healthy structures.

Our leadership team has a concern to make an adequate expression of church available to every believer, even as we actively promote fresh and innovative "wineskins" for the church. In our passion to see new expressions of church and a multiplication movement, we do not want to oversimplify and dilute Christ's description of his church.

Our goal is not to prescribe what a definition of "church" should be or a universal minimum ecclesiology. We simply believe it's critically important to consider how the following elements fit in your ecclesiology. That's why we've developed the following questions to help you decide on a minimum ecclesiology grounded in history and God's Word:

1. Biblical Instruction — What does the Bible say about church?

2. Biblical Example — What practices are at play in the Bible narrative?

3. Church Fathers — What teachings and practices do we see in the Early Church Fathers' writings?

4. Cultural Sensitivity — How can we be sensitive to different cultural contexts without compromising core biblical truths, teachings, and intentions?

As you look at these four considerations, your ecclesiology will begin to emerge around baseline doctrines, practices, and governance.

1. Doctrines — What are the essential beliefs of the church?

   For example:

   - The Father is worshipped as creator.

   - Jesus is exalted and confessed as Savior and Lord.

   - The Spirit is honored as present and active.

   - The Scriptures are authoritative for life and doctrine.

2. Functions — What are the essential practices of the church?

   For example:

   - Worship
   - Teaching
   - Prayer
   - Sacraments
   - Fellowship
   - Disciple-making
   - Compassion
   - Justice
   - Mission
   - Global missions
   - Body ministry

3. Governance — What are the essential structures, leaders, and accountability practices of the church?

   For example:

   - Elders
   - Pastors
   - Deacons
   - Apostles
   - Prophets
   - Evangelists
   - Shepherds
   - Teachers
   - Church councils
   - Moral standards
   - Church discipline
   - Church boards

With that backdrop in view, a plethora of definitions for the essential traits of a biblical church have been offered by scores of theologians, pastors, and Christian leaders.

Below are four examples of a minimum ecclesiology from four different sources. These are the irreducible characteristics of church. One comes from the Exponential team, one from a denomination in light of their new emphasis on church planting, one from a historic confession, and one from a missional author. These are meant to help you think toward what your church's (or tribe's) minimal ecclesiology will be:

Exponential's Description of the Irreducible Traits of a Biblical Church

When we search the New Testament to identify the characteristics which constituted the first century church, the following summation is an example that surfaces.

"Church" is happening when these seven traits are recognizable in a gathering:

1. **Jesus is worshipped as Lord.**

   - The gathered believers are united in loving fellowship around the *Trinitarian* presence of the one true God: the Father, the Son Jesus Christ, and the Holy Spirit.

   - Jesus is honored as the incarnation of God and *foundation/cornerstone* of the church.

   - *Worship* in any of its multiple forms (prayer, singing, giving, etc.) is happening.

   - Jesus is acknowledged as the ultimate authority, leader, and *head* of the church (Lord).

   - Jesus is honored as *present* when a group (even two or three) gather in his name.

2. **Scripture is taught and obeyed as truth.**

   - The Scriptures are honored as the *authority* in all matters of *doctrine* and *life*.

   - The Scriptures are *read* and *shared* as the directive of the faith community.

- The Scriptures provide a *moral authority* which imparts a standard of conduct to the community.

- The Scriptures define and prioritize individual and corporate *holiness.*

3. Believers gather regularly for fellowship and prayer.

- The church is made up of "*believers*" — those who have been born again into her.

- The church is *interdependent individuals* (the people of God) who assemble for spiritual purposes.

- The *assembling* of a defined group of believers happens *frequently* enough to advance the interactive realities of behaving as a *family.*

- Fellowship, "*koinonia,*" the "joint sharing together in Christ," is occurring in the gathering.

- The "*one another*" passages of Scripture are practiced as a fulfillment of "fellowship."

- Active *love* and *mutuality,* caring for the needs of one another, is prioritized.

- *Unity* of the faith and spirit overcome divisions caused by race, class, status, or gender.

- *Prayer* for one another is a defining practice of the fellowship.

4. Sacraments are practiced.

- *Prayer* is an active and vital ritual of the church.

- *Baptism* is practiced for initiating believers into the church.

- *Communion/*The Lord's Supper is practiced as an ongoing remembrance of the reality and centrality of Christ's salvific work.

5. Spiritual authority is present, credible, and active.

- *Overseers and leaders* (elders, deacons, apostles, prophets, evangelists, shepherds, teachers) are established in a credible manner.

- Overseers and leaders *teach* and *equip* the saints for maturity, ministry, and mission.

- *Church discipline* is exercised to guard the church and aid the individual believer.

6. God's mission of disciple-making and servanthood are core priorities.

- The church understands itself as an expression of God's *kingdom mission*.

- The *Great Commission (going and making disciples)* is prioritized and practiced.

- *Serving in missional practices* is prioritized and practiced.

- *Evangelism* is prioritized and viewed as the first step in disciple-making.

- The *priesthood of all believers* shapes how the church pursues the mission.

- *Intercessory prayer and fasting* is practiced as a primary means of mission advancement.

7. The Presence of the Spirit is active in the gathering.

- The Spirit is *empowering* the fruit and gifts of the Spirit.

- The Spirit is *teaching* the gathered believers.

- The Spirit is *comforting and guiding* the church.

Note: All of these seven traits are observable on some tangible level (except, perhaps, the seventh) thus allowing evaluation of their presence. This description leaves ample room for the variety of practices, forms of governance, and diverse doctrines present in the church today. Yet if any of these seven essential attributes are not present to some degree, then the "gathering" has probably not matured into a "local church." (See the Appendix at the end for corresponding Scriptures.)

Wesleyan Description of the Irreducible Traits of a Biblical Church[20]

A denominational example: As the Wesleyan denomination has recently moved forward in church planting and innovative forms of church gatherings, they deemed it important to produce a new statement of their essential ecclesiology.

Here's their list of questions for identifying markers of the church:

- Are disciples being equipped to make disciples (Matthew 28:19-20)?

- Are believers set apart as holy for a special purpose by and for God, thus equipping them to understand and utilize their spiritual gifts (Ephesians 4:11-16; Romans 12:6-8)?

- Is there an accountability structure to implement church governance and discipline, to ensure correct doctrine is followed (Matthew 18:15-20; 2 Timothy 3:16; 2 Peter 2:1-22)?

- Are there celebrations and stories of individuals committing to follow Christ and being baptized (2 Peter 3:8-10; Romans 6:4)?

- Is there intentional progress toward sending out leaders and reproducing new churches (Acts 1:8)?

- Are there forms of outward-oriented witness to act justly, love mercy, and walk humbly into communities that are nearby, hard to reach, or faraway around the globe (Micah 6:8; Matthew 5:16; Acts 1:8)?

- Are the gathered believers united in loving fellowship around the Trinitarian presence of God: the Father, the Son Jesus Christ and the Holy Spirit (Matthew 28:19-20)?

- Are times of prayer, teaching of the Word of God and the Lord's Supper all meaningful parts of church gatherings resulting in a loving witness to the world (Acts 2:42; Romans 12:1-2; Philippians 2:5; 1 John 4:11-12)?

- Are there regular gatherings so that believers might band together to study and apply the Bible to their lives (Acts 2:42; Romans 12:1-2; Matthew 6:33; Hebrews 10:25; 2 Timothy 3:16; Luke 22:14-23)?

- Are nonbelievers welcomed into relationships with believers and church gatherings so they might respond to the saving message of Jesus Christ and enter into the kingdom of God (Romans 1:16, 6:1-4, 10:14; 1 Corinthians 15:23; Matthew 28:19-20)?

Belgic Confession Description of the Irreducible Traits of a Biblical Church

A historic example: *The Belgic Confession* devotes a chapter (Article 29) to the "Marks of the True Church":

The true church can be recognized if it has the following marks:

1. The church engages in the pure preaching of the gospel;

2. The church makes use of the pure administration of the sacraments as Christ instituted them;

3. The church practices church discipline for correcting faults;

4. The church governs itself according to the pure Word of God, rejecting all things contrary to it and holding Jesus Christ as the only Head.

By these marks one can be assured of recognizing the true church — and no one ought to be separated from it.[21]

Alan Hirsch's Description of the Irreducible Traits of a Biblical Church

In his influential book *The Forgotten Ways: Reactivating the Missional Church*, author Alan Hirsch offers five essential marks of biblical ecclesiology to help us recover the "genius of the apostolic church":[22]

1. Christ is the Center (God-focused)

2. Christ is continually being reproduced (disciple-making)

3. Christ manifests his love through the members (compassionate communion)

4. Christ works through every believer in the Body (universal priesthood)

5. Christ redeems the whole of creation through the church (outward mission)

Clarity of Ecclesiology

For the mobilization flywheel to turn effectively, it must embrace a simple, but not simplistic, ecclesiology. It must pursue a simple church model without offering less than a biblical church. The understanding of church must be robust enough to promote long-term health and the reproduction of the disciple, the gathering, and the church. It must be adaptive enough to shape itself to every changing cultural reality without compromising its essence. We anticipate and encourage creative shapes and styles of churches to reach our mission field while maintaining true church identity.

The sharper this ecclesiastical focus is, the more likely the church will hit God's missional bullseye for the church. There are a variety of factors that will combine to influence the ecclesiastical definition for the local church. For many, the particular tribe, denomination, or network they belong to will be the key factor in their understanding of the church. These "tribes" can be either a significant help or a hindrance to the turning of the flywheel. We consider these "tribes" in the next chapter.

CHAPTER 7

The Tribe: Shaping the Impact of Networks & Denominations

Denominations, Networks, and Associations Create Cultures and Systems which either accelerate or decelerate the mobilization of disciples and multiplication of churches.

THE TRIBE

In recent years, I've noticed that church plants have become a bit like NASCAR racecars. These vehicles usually carry sponsorship from several companies. The primary sponsor gets the hood and gets to choose the car's color. The other sponsors pay varying prices for the placement of their stickers on the racecar. There is typically a relationship between the sticker on the car and the company behind the sticker.

Denominations, associations, or networks often sponsor church plants and invest in them. It is not unusual these days to also have a few different networks putting their sticker on a church plant. Generally, these stickers and the relationships behind them are a significant advantage to the church plants. Occasionally, however, the sponsors/coaches/overseers can become encumbrances. It is vital to the mobilization flywheel that these "tribes" act as oil and don't become sand in the gears.

Denominations, associations and networks create cultures and systems that either accelerate or decelerate the mobilization of disciples and the multiplication of churches.

Building the Mobilization Flywheel:
100% of churches can become mobilization stations that equip and send believers.
100% of believers have the calling and ability to be everyday missionaries where they live, work, or play.
100% of everyday missionaries can play a role in gatherings.
Most everyday missionaries can form and lead a gathering of seekers or believers.

Many gatherings can become new churches led by everyday missionaries (who are predominately bi-vocational).

This mobilization process is helped or hindered by the criteria set by your church, denomination, or tribe.

100% of these new churches can be "biblically defined churches."

100% of denominations and networks (tribes) can provide support to the flywheel.

As the mobilization flywheel turns, it can create not only individual churches but also groups of churches. Often these new churches are already attached to a particular denomination through the parent church. Alternately, these new churches may become a part of a denomination or network or both. Occasionally, the mobilization flywheel will create a group of churches who become their own network or denomination (such as Hillsong or Vineyard). These collectives of churches hold much potential for kingdom advancement. Groupings of churches are capable of doing far more together than they can alone.

Denominations are accelerators to the mission of God when they synergistically bring together resources to meet needs and accomplish mission. They act as the body of Christ on a broader scale than an individual local church. They offer the gifts and strengths of their local church to their larger family of churches. In addition, healthy denominations reach beyond themselves to other denominations to collectively accomplish kingdom work, despite differences on secondary issues.

"Denominationalism," on the other hand, is a form of exclusivism and is a deterrent to the mission of God. Denominationalism is marked by an air of superiority, instead of servanthood, and divides the universal church due to secondary doctrines.

Networks and denominations create structures, systems, norms, expectations, and relationships, which either accelerate or decelerate the mobilization of disciples and the multiplication of churches.

The Two Cans

"Tribes" hold two cans in their hands — one contains gas and the other water.

When a flame of the Spirit ignites one of their pastors or churches, denominations or networks usually hasten to either feed the flame with fuel or extinguish it with water. The fueling of the flame comes from intentional efforts to support new gatherings and churches with prayer, resources, finances, counseling, administrative services, etc. Often the "watering" of the flame is done unintentionally and even unconsciously. The water comes in the form of structure, systems, expectations, rules, politics, legalities, etc.

Acts 15 speaks to these two paths created by church authority. The church in Jerusalem and the church in Antioch were quite different in some significant ways. When some came from Judea to Antioch promoting divergent thinking on a primary doctrinal and missional issue, a sharp division arose. The Antioch church sent Paul and Barnabas to Jerusalem. Once there, they "reported" to those they deemed as their authority — "the apostles and elders" (Acts 15:4).

The leaders of the Jerusalem church were confronted with the choice of imposing complexity or endorsing simplicity, of choosing the "can of gas" or the "can of water" for the flame of Paul's ministry. James declared that those who had "troubled" the Antioch church with their teaching "went without our authorization" (Acts 15:24). This is a clear statement of authority and accountability within the broader church network — an authority Paul honored.

James then gave the decision of the Jerusalem church council: "It is my judgment, therefore, that we should not make it difficult for the Gentiles who are turning to God" (Acts 15:19). "It seemed good to the Holy Spirit and to us not to burden you with anything beyond the following requirements" (Acts 15:28).

The council decided to use the can of fuel.

The result of this collaboration between the Jerusalem and Antioch church was increased fruit and accelerated mission for the kingdom. Acts 16:4-5 reports,

> As they traveled from town to town, they delivered the decisions reached by the apostles and elders in Jerusalem for the people to obey. So the churches were strengthened in the faith and grew daily in numbers.

The church leadership in Jerusalem poured gas on the fire of the Holy Spirit's work among the churches. Sadly, the opposite is often true in denominations and networks.

The Progression from Revival to Institution

Often (with some notable exceptions) kingdom work usually proceeds as follows:

1. **Personal or Local Church Revival**

   A person receives an extraordinary encounter with God and a flame for God's mission is ignited. They become radically contagious with the gospel and begin to spread the fire. Examples are people like the apostle Paul, John Wesley, Billy Graham, and Ralph Moore. Occasionally, the Spirit will peculiarly grip a small group or local church, a fire will lite and begin to propagate this flame. Think Azusa Street, Cane Ridge Revival, and Asbury College.

2. **Movement**

   As the flame of the Spirit passes from one person to the next, a growing collective of people coalesces. Many burning hearts begin moving on mission in the same direction with significant kingdom impact. Sparks are flying everywhere, igniting new fires. There is no progressive systematized plan or strategy being carefully followed. Missionaries are reaching their local context with effectiveness or are being called to unusual places to take the flame there also — or both. New groups are being raised up who share the passion for this fresh work God is doing. From these groups, new churches begin springing to life in a variety of places.

3. **Organization**

   As the movement expands and ages, there develops a need to bring a level of organization to the various moving parts. What has occurred spontaneously needs to be developed, defined, protected and made (to the degree it can be) transferable. The further out the mission goes, the greater the likelihood of mission and doctrine dilution or corruption. Effective organizing allows the movement to mature, stay healthy, create sustainability, increase impact, and spark new movements. The focus remains on the movement and the individuals on the edges who are driving and leading the movement.

4. Institution

As the movement becomes more ordered, there is often a subtle yet deadly shift to prioritizing the created organization above the mission which the structure was created to serve. There are moves to preserve and protect what has already been accomplished. Inside stakeholders are valued higher than outsiders in need. The emphasis transitions from the external mission to more finely tuned internal processes, policies, and definitions. Long-term financial stability is prioritized over shorter-term mission accomplishment. The original "why" of the mission gets lost in the "how," "what," and "who" of the institution.

5. Museum

As the movement dies, it leaves behind only the shell of the institution to which it gave birth. The institution is preserved by consuming the resources the initial movement generated. The only energy for the institutional museum is found in curating the past and telling "glory stories" of what the movement used to be.

To summarize the phases of change:

- Revivals/renewals *initiate* change.

- Movements *propel* change.

- Organizations *sustain* change.

- Institutions *resist* change.

- If we're not careful to follow God, institutions become museums that *memorialize* change.

Consequently, the church must continuously be renewing itself by seeking revival, feeding movement, loosely organizing momentum, resisting institutionalism, and closing museums. How do tribes avoid this life-sucking, downward spiral? How do they feed the fire instead of quenching the flame?

Tribes can embrace the "chaordic" nature of Spirit-led movements.

"Chaordic" blends the words "chaos" and "order." First coined by Dee Hock, the founder and former CEO of the Visa credit card company, "chaordic" describes the creative and productive intersection between chaos and order.[23]

Envision three overlapping circles in this order: chaos, order, and control. "Management" happens at the overlap between order and control. Most pastors, tribal leaders, and organizations love control and eschew chaos. Consequently, they move toward over-control. This kills innovation and inspiration. It also chases away the Holy Spirit as they rely on programs more than on "power."

Conversely, "leadership" happens at the overlap between chaos and order. It empowers creativity, spontaneity, and individuality. It creates space for the Holy Spirit to work in fresh and new ways.

Tribes must be willing to move to "chaordic" to initiate and sustain movement. The book of Acts seems resplendent with chaordic structure-empowering movements.

For example:

- Barnabas carefully teaches Jesus in Antioch as a representative of the Jerusalem church; then the Spirit sends him to find the former Christian-killer Saul in Tarsus.

- Stephen systematically orders food for the widows; then does astounding miracles in Jesus name.

- Philip runs beside chariots before carefully explaining Scripture, before being Spirit-transported to Azotus.

- Paul free-wheels for the gospel but comes back to Jerusalem to check in.

- Some Jesus followers flee the persecution in Jerusalem and travel to Cyprus and Cyrene sharing the gospel but only with the Jews. Then they feel led to Antioch. When they get there, they start sharing it with the Greeks and a bunch of them get saved.

- The Spirit tells the Antioch church to send Paul and Barnabas on their first church-planting journey, so they do — without even checking in with Jerusalem.

The church in Acts clearly has structure. But it is so decentralized, permission-giving, and empowering that you never know where or how it's going to break out next.

When denominations over-complicate ecclesiology or over-educate ordination, or over-control churches for the sake of "brand" purity, then movement becomes difficult to mobilize, if not impossible.

Tribes can zealously listen and serve, rather than mandate and be served.

Tribes must maintain their priority on "frontline" ministry.

As an organization grows or ages, it is too easy to ...

- Switch the priority from the local church's mission goals to the organization's goals

- Leverage the energy and resources of the local church to serve the organization's needs

- Consume too large of a percentage of the finances or time in the maintenance of the organization — organizations are adept at creating ever-increasing overhead

- Impose global vision rather than support local vision

- Create reporting structures that become cumbersome and counterproductive

- Cannibalize the best apostolic and evangelistic leaders, inviting them to serve in more lucrative and organizationally prominent political positions, which often are primarily bureaucratic

Any of these shifts will begin to quench the fire of movement.

Tribes can focus on their areas of highest contribution.

There are some key resources that tribes have to offer to the mobilization flywheel. The concept of "better together" is especially possible when it comes to advantages that a tribe can offer to a local church. The following are twelve unique contributions that tribes are best positioned to provide:

Culture – Tribes can foster a culture that stresses mobilizing believers, creating missional communities, and planting new churches; incubating positive peer pressure around kingdom priorities instead of rewarding short-sighted "addition-only" thinking; promoting a tribal scoreboard around mobilization and multiplication.

Accountability – Provide an outside source of accountability for the character and teaching of those planting new churches. Paul told Timothy, "Watch your life and doctrine closely. Persevere in them, because if you do, you will save both yourself and your hearers" (1 Tim. 4:16). Paul was going to be one source for that accountability. Tribes can help deal with doctrinal outliers before they become heretical. They can help stop wolves in sheep's clothing.

Relationships — Provide personal encouragement to leaders, pastors, missionaries, planters, and their spouses. They can connect ministers and leaders together who can support one another. These leaders may otherwise be unaware of one another.

Inspiration — Tribes have convening power that can not only breathe life into the movement as a whole but can also inspire individual ministers. These larger gatherings can provide a broader motivational and visionary context for the local work.

Spiritual — Provide spiritual covering and mobilize national prayer networks. Healthy spiritual authority can engage in prayers and actions of spiritual protection on behalf of the churches they oversee. The Book of Acts and the Epistles are filled with references of apostolic prayers on behalf of local ministers, churches, and groups of churches. Galvanizing intercessors on behalf of movements is of inestimable value.

Coaching — Provide a network of coaches to come alongside the missionaries and ministers to mentor them into increased effectiveness. Also, delivering resources such as classes, continuing education, curriculum, on-line forums, webinars, etc. can provide workers and leaders the tools to produce greater fruitfulness.

Credibility — Communicate national affiliation in the local context and provide name recognition. When new works are associated with a broader and established group, more legitimacy is immediately conferred. People in the community with previous exposure to a particular denomination or network in their past can locate and connect with the new expression.

Personnel — Assist in locating student workers, interns, residents, short-term missionaries, and staff. Help provide new leaders who can increase effectiveness.

Financial — Provide partnership funding for expenses through grants and networking. Tribes can help a local church reach beyond themselves in fundraising, through both the ability to reach a larger number of interested individuals and through connecting with high-income donors. Denominations and networks can highly prioritize and pour resources into the frontline work of mobilization and multiplication. The collective strength of a larger group of churches gives local churches access to financial instruments (such as investments, pensions, and loans), which they otherwise would not have.

Property — Assist in the acquisition of property. Often tribes can provide financing or provide the financial credibility or backing for loans for new works. Tribes also frequently have expertise within their ranks who can provide a necessary skill or knowledge the local church does not have.

Administrative — By centralizing certain administrative tasks, tribes can partner with local churches so ministers do not become bogged down with the administrivia but are freed to primarily focus on missional priorities.

Legal / Insurance — In a litigious society, churches are more frequently becoming a legal target for those opposing the gospel. Tribes can assist new churches in legal compliance and insurance provision.

Paul writes of the tribal nature of the church in 1 Thessalonians 2:14: "For you, brothers and sisters, became imitators of God's churches in Judea, which are in Christ Jesus: You suffered from your own people the same things those churches suffered from the Jews."

The church at Thessalonica learned, grew, and endured from imitating the churches in Judea. The local church of Thessalonica was comforted and strengthened because of their relationship with their sister churches in Judea.

This is God's desire that his churches would be joined together for the sake of the gospel and the sake of those carrying the gospel. Tribes who know how to bring churches together while feeding the flames of the gospel movement will flourish.

Questions to Consider

- Can churches accomplish more kingdom work through collaboration than through independence or isolation?

- Can a group of likeminded churches provide support and accountability for one another?

- Can networks or denominations provide resourcing beyond what independent churches are capable of?

- Should networks and denominations prioritize the mission of the local church over the life of the organization/institution?

- Who can bury people? Can the ordinary Jesus-follower in your church perform funerals?

CONCLUSION

God's Movement Through a Mobilized Church

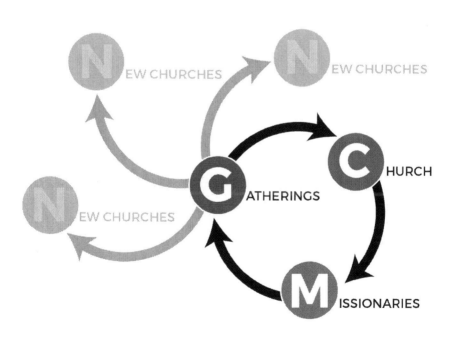

GOD'S MOVEMENT THROUGH A MOBILIZED CHURCH

The mobilization flywheel has the potential to power the church forward into the complex reality of twenty-first century culture. It is what will allow the gospel to reach into every diverse nook and cranny of society.

The mobilization flywheel can unleash a fresh new revolution of evangelism, discipleship, and church multiplication. But we must freshly understand the meaning of "mobilize." As we mentioned above, the definition of mobilize is important:

> **mo·bi·lize** – 1) prepare and organize for active service, 2) make something movable or capable of movement

The church must organize itself for active service so it can make something (i.e., the gospel) capable of movement! The Spirit has already prepared us for being mobilized.

Movements in the kingdom always gain inspiration and energy from the Holy Spirit. Similarly, a flywheel always requires something to get the ball rolling. That's what the Spirit does for mobilization: it gives the spark and fans the flames of the movements of God. The fire of the Spirit in Acts 2 came to the one hundred twenty believers in a most interesting manner. It began as a bonfire in the middle of the room but then separated into distinct flames that came to rest upon every single one of the one hundred twenty! One hundred percent of them were filled with the Holy Spirit, and each of them began to proclaim God's wonders. No one was looking at Peter or James or Mary and saying, "We are counting on you to carry the flame!" Why? Because each of them had their own individual flame. They were each empowered for ministry.

Sadly, for too long believers have delegated the flame to those they deem more deserving, more trained, more holy, more gifted, or more knowledgeable. They have reclined in the upper room instead of taking their flame out to the streets where the Spirit was leading them. They have stayed inside the church, singing about God's relentless love for them, instead of letting God's love send them to relentlessly share it with those outside the church.

But Christians were *made for more*! The church was *made for more*!

The mission to reach our nation with the gospel is far beyond the reach of the church as she is doing ministry today. But there is a growing discontent with "Church, Inc.," with spectator church, with consumeristic Christians, with easy believism. People want to get off the bench, out of the huddle, and onto the scrimmage line. There is a fresh wind of the Spirit, new voices being lifted up, new hands being placed on the mobilization flywheel, and they starting to turn it.

Requirements of the Mobilization Flywheel

To summarize what we've covered in this book, the mobilization flywheel requires:

Churches — Churches that adopt and practice a multiplication mindset that emphasizes "sending." They see their ordinary attendees as capable of accomplishing significant kingdom ministry. These churches prioritize helping members live into their calling outside the church more than inside the church.

These churches are raising up everyday missionaries, not just volunteers for ministry. Consequently, they seek to keep the church simple and mission-focused so the "machine" doesn't consume too much of their member's time, thus becoming competitive with their member's mission work outside the church. The leaders of these churches understand their primary ministry role is not running programs but equipping members to reach and disciple people in their individual mission field.

Everyday missionaries — These individual believers have had their self-image transformed by the power of the gospel. They understand themselves as saved, called, and empowered by the Spirit for mission and ministry. The "priesthood of all believers" is not a nebulous theological concept for them but a daily reality as they reconcile people in their world with God.

These everyday missionaries recognize their general calling and are living into that daily. At the same time, they are seeking to know and live out their specific calling. They are keenly aware of people where they work, live, study, and play; these comprise their unique mission field. They have identified their particular "circle of influence" and are earnestly praying for those in it. The daily witness of their lifestyle and the frequent verbal sharing of Christ is impacting lives and winning converts. These converts are being discipled in biblical, relational, obedience-based discipleship models.

Gatherings — The assembling together of a small to midsize group for fellowship, growth, and mission. As everyday missionaries are helping people in their circle of influence toward a growing relationship with Jesus, missionaries begin to collect these individuals together for accelerating spiritual growth and creating a group identity.

These gatherings begin to host the practice of the "one another" passages of Scripture, the exercise of spiritual gifts, intercessory prayer, and mission discernment and engagement. Individual believers mature spiritually as they receive from and give to others. These gatherings often begin to develop a vision for their collective ministry together.

New churches — Some of these gatherings will develop into new churches, while others will reproduce themselves and strengthen the existing church of which they are a part. As gatherings mature, they will begin to develop more leadership and more spiritual practices, which may lead to their becoming an identifiable local church.

These new churches will have a strong culture of mobilization and often have bi-vocational or co-vocational pastors. These new churches will birth new flywheels of multiplication.

If we have:

- Churches raising up and equipping missionaries instead of volunteers;

- Everyday missionaries bringing Jesus everywhere they live, work, and play;

- Disciples being brought into community in faith-based gatherings;

- Gatherings becoming new churches or planting new churches;

- New churches operating biblically and mobilizing their members to go serve; and

- Tribes pouring fuel on the flames of the Spirit in local churches;

Then we will have stories of revival, harvest, and movements reaching millions and changing nations!

This is what we believe the mobilization flywheel can unleash within the church.

May God's grace help us turn the wheel that mobilizes and multiplies the church of Jesus because Christ — through everyday missionaries who are making disciples and building the local church — is the hope of the world.

Recommended next steps of action:

1. Have your team read through Ephesians and Acts, with a focus on the theme of mobilization.

2. Have your team read through the "Made for More Visual Guide" (a free download from Exponential at exponential.org/resources).

3. Have your team work through the *Made for More Resource Kit* (a free download at exponential.net/register/made-resource-kit).

4. Take the online Mobilization Culture Assessment (available starting February 1, 2019).

5. Attend the Exponential National Conference or one of Exponential's regional conferences where the focus is on mobilization — or both.

APPENDIX

Scriptures on Essential Ecclesiology

Exponential's Irreducible Traits of a Biblical Church with Scriptures

In an effort to provide scriptural support as a resource for the reader, we have quoted Scriptures that undergird each essential trait we listed in Chapter 6. Again, Exponential provides this list of traits as one possible example of minimal ecclesiology. We believe each tribe must create their own definition, and we seek to serve all tribes who are building God's church.

A gathering can be identified as a church when we find the following seven traits:

1. **Jesus is worshipped as Lord.**

   1 Corinthians 1:2: "To the church of God in Corinth, to those sanctified in Christ Jesus and called to be his holy people, together with all those everywhere who call on the name of our Lord Jesus Christ — their Lord and ours."

   Philippians 2:9-11: "Therefore God exalted him to the highest place and gave him the name that is above every name, that at the name of Jesus every knee should bow, in heaven and on earth and under the earth, and every tongue acknowledge that Jesus Christ is Lord, to the glory of God the Father."

   Romans 10:9: "If you declare with your mouth, 'Jesus is Lord,' and believe in your heart that God raised him from the dead, you will be saved."

- The gathered believers are united in loving fellowship around the Trinitarian presence of the one true God: The Father, the Son Jesus Christ, and the Holy Spirit.

  Matthew 28:19: "Therefore go and make disciples of all nations, baptizing them in the name of the Father and of the Son and of the Holy Spirit."

  John 14:26: "But the Advocate, the Holy Spirit, whom the Father will send in my name, will teach you all things and will remind you of everything I have said to you."

- Jesus is honored as the incarnation of God and the foundation/cornerstone of the church.

  Colossians 2:9: "For in Christ all the fullness of the Deity lives in bodily form."

  Colossians 1:15, 18: "The Son is the image of the invisible God, the firstborn over all creation. ... And he is the head of the body, the church; he is the beginning and the firstborn from among the dead, so that in everything he might have the supremacy."

  Matthew 16:18: "And I tell you that you are Peter, and on this rock I will build my church, and the gates of Hades will not overcome it."

  Ephesians 2:19-20: "Consequently, you are no longer foreigners and strangers, but fellow citizens with God's people and also members of his household, built on the foundation of the apostles and prophets, with Christ Jesus himself as the chief cornerstone."

- The act(s) of worship in any of its multiple forms (prayer, singing, etc.) is happening.

  Hebrews 13:15: "Through Jesus, therefore, let us continually offer to God a sacrifice of praise — the fruit of lips that openly profess his name."

  Colossians 3:16-17: "Let the message of Christ dwell among you richly as you teach and admonish one another with all wisdom through psalms, hymns, and songs from the Spirit, singing to God with gratitude in your hearts. And whatever you do, whether in word or deed, do it all in the name of the Lord Jesus, giving thanks to God the Father through him."

1 Peter 2:5: "You also, like living stones, are being built into a spiritual house to be a holy priesthood, offering spiritual sacrifices acceptable to God through Jesus Christ."

- ○ **Jesus is the head of the church (Lord) as the authority and ultimate leader.**

  Ephesians 1:22: "And God placed all things under his feet and appointed him to be head over everything for the church."

  Ephesians 4:15: "Instead, speaking the truth in love, we will grow to become in every respect the mature body of him who is the head, that is, Christ."

  Colossians 1:18: "And he is the head of the body, the church; he is the beginning and the firstborn from among the dead, so that in everything he might have the supremacy."

- ○ **Jesus is present when a group (even two or three) gathers in his name.**

  Matthew 18:20: "For where two or three gather in my name, there am I with them."

  Revelation 2:1: "To the angel of the church in Ephesus write: These are the words of him who holds the seven stars in his right hand and walks among the seven golden lampstands."

2. Scripture is taught and obeyed as truth.

Acts 2:42: "They devoted themselves to the apostles' teaching and to fellowship, to the breaking of bread and to prayer."

- ○ **The Scriptures are the authority in all matters of doctrine and life.**

  1 Corinthians 15:3-4: "For what I received I passed on to you as of first importance: that Christ died for our sins according to the Scriptures, that he was buried, that he was raised on the third day according to the Scriptures."

2 Timothy 3:15: "And how from infancy you have known the Holy Scriptures, which are able to make you wise for salvation through faith in Christ Jesus."

2 Peter 3:16: "He writes the same way in all his letters, speaking in them of these matters. His letters contain some things that are hard to understand, which ignorant and unstable people distort, as they do the other Scriptures, to their own destruction."

○ **The Scriptures are read and shared as the directive of the faith community.**

1 Timothy 4:13,16: "Until I come, devote yourself to the public reading of Scripture, to preaching and to teaching. ... Watch your life and doctrine closely. Persevere in them, because if you do, you will save both yourself and your hearers."

○ **The Scriptures provide a moral authority that imparts a standard of conduct to the community.**

2 Timothy 3:16-17: "All Scripture is God-breathed and is useful for teaching, rebuking, correcting and training in righteousness, so that the servant of God may be thoroughly equipped for every good work."

○ **The Scriptures define and prioritize individual and corporate holiness.**

1 Corinthians 1:2: "To the church of God in Corinth, to those sanctified in Christ Jesus and called to be his holy people, together with all those everywhere who call on the name of our Lord Jesus Christ — their Lord and ours."

Ephesians 2:21: "In him the whole building is joined together and rises to become a holy temple in the Lord."

3. **Believers gather regularly for fellowship and prayer.**

Acts 2:42: "They devoted themselves to the apostles' teaching and to fellowship, to the breaking of bread and to prayer."

Hebrews 10:24-25: "And let us consider how we may spur one another on toward love and good deeds, not giving up meeting together, as some are in the habit of doing, but encouraging one another — and all the more as you see the Day approaching."

- ○ **The church is made up of "believers," those who have been born again into her.**

  1 Peter 2:17: "Show proper respect to everyone, love the family of believers, fear God, honor the emperor."

  1 Peter 5:9: "Resist him, standing firm in the faith, because you know that the family of believers throughout the world is undergoing the same kind of sufferings."

- ○ **The church is interdependent believers (the people of God) who assemble for spiritual purposes.**

  Romans 12:4-6: "For just as each of us has one body with many members, and these members do not all have the same function, so in Christ we, though many, form one body, and each member belongs to all the others. We have different gifts, according to the grace given to each of us. If your gift is prophesying, then prophesy in accordance with your faith."

- ○ **The assembling of a defined group of believers happens frequently enough to advance the interactive realities of behaving as a family.**

  1 Corinthians 14:26: "What then shall we say, brothers and sisters? When you come together, each of you has a hymn, or a word of instruction, a revelation, a tongue or an interpretation. Everything must be done so that the church may be built up."

- ○ **Fellowship, "koinonia," the "joint sharing together in Christ," is occurring in the gathering.**

  1 John 1:3, 7: "We proclaim to you what we have seen and heard, so that you also may have fellowship with us. And our fellowship is with the Father and with his Son, Jesus Christ. ... But if we walk in the light, as he is in the light, we have fellowship with one another, and the blood of Jesus, his Son, purifies us from all sin."

- ○ **The "one another" passages of Scripture are practiced as a fulfillment of "fellowship."**

  Romans 12:10: "Be devoted to one another in love. Honor one another above yourselves."

  Ephesians 5:21: "Submit to one another out of reverence for Christ."

- ○ **Active love and mutuality, caring for the needs of one another, is prioritized.**

  Acts 2:44-45: "All the believers were together and had everything in common. They sold property and possessions to give to anyone who had need."

  Acts 4:34-35: "That there were no needy persons among them. For from time to time those who owned land or houses sold them, brought the money from the sales and put it at the apostles' feet, and it was distributed to anyone who had need."

- ○ **Unity of the faith and spirit overcome divisions caused by race, class, gender.**

  Galatians 3:26-28: "So in Christ Jesus you are all children of God through faith, for all of you who were baptized into Christ have clothed yourselves with Christ. There is neither Jew nor Gentile, neither slave nor free, nor is there male and female, for you are all one in Christ Jesus."

- ○ **Prayer is a defining practice of the fellowship.**

  Acts 2:42: "They devoted themselves to the apostles' teaching and to fellowship, to the breaking of bread and to prayer."

  Acts 12:5: "So Peter was kept in prison, but the church was earnestly praying to God for him."

  Colossians 4:2: "Devote yourselves to prayer, being watchful and thankful."

  James 5:16: "Therefore confess your sins to each other and pray for each other so that you may be healed. The prayer of a righteous person is powerful and effective."

4. Sacraments are practiced.

○ **Prayer is an active and vital ritual of the church.**

Acts 2:42: "They devoted themselves to the apostles' teaching and to fellowship, to the breaking of bread and to prayer."

Acts 6:4: " ... and will give our attention to prayer and the ministry of the word."

Acts 14:23: "Paul and Barnabas appointed elders for them in each church and, with prayer and fasting, committed them to the Lord, in whom they had put their trust."

Colossians 4:2: "Devote yourselves to prayer, being watchful and thankful."

James 5:14-16: "Is anyone among you sick? Let them call the elders of the church to pray over them and anoint them with oil in the name of the Lord. And the prayer offered in faith will make the sick person well; the Lord will raise them up. If they have sinned, they will be forgiven. Therefore confess your sins to each other and pray for each other so that you may be healed. The prayer of a righteous person is powerful and effective."

○ **Baptism into the church is practiced.**

Acts 2:38, 41: "Peter replied, 'Repent and be baptized, every one of you, in the name of Jesus Christ for the forgiveness of your sins. And you will receive the gift of the Holy Spirit.' ... Those who accepted his message were baptized, and about three thousand were added to their number that day."

1 Corinthians 12:13: "For we were all baptized by one Spirit so as to form one body — whether Jews or Gentiles, slave or free — and we were all given the one Spirit to drink."

Ephesians 4:4-5: "There is one body and one Spirit, just as you were called to one hope when you were called; one Lord, one faith, one baptism."

- ○ **Communion/The Lord's Supper is practiced as an ongoing remembrance of the reality and centrality of Christ's salvific work.**

  Acts 2:42: "They devoted themselves to the apostles' teaching and to fellowship, to the breaking of bread [communion] and to prayer."

  1 Corinthians 11:23-26: "For I received from the Lord what I also passed on to you: The Lord Jesus, on the night he was betrayed, took bread, and when he had given thanks, he broke it and said, 'This is my body, which is for you; do this in remembrance of me.' In the same way, after supper he took the cup, saying, 'This cup is the new covenant in my blood; do this, whenever you drink it, in remembrance of me.' For whenever you eat this bread and drink this cup, you proclaim the Lord's death until he comes."

5. **Spiritual authority is present, credible, and active.**

   Hebrews 13:17: "Have confidence in your leaders and submit to their authority, because they keep watch over you as those who must give an account. Do this so that their work will be a joy, not a burden, for that would be of no benefit to you."

   - ○ **Overseers and leaders (elders, deacons, apostles, prophets, evangelists, shepherds, teachers) are established in a credible manner.**

     Acts 14:23: "Paul and Barnabas appointed elders for them in each church and, with prayer and fasting, committed them to the Lord, in whom they had put their trust."

     Acts 15:6: "The apostles and elders met to consider this question."

     Acts 20:28: "Keep watch over yourselves and all the flock of which the Holy Spirit has made you overseers. Be shepherds of the church of God, which he bought with his own blood."

     1 Timothy 5:17: "The elders who direct the affairs of the church well are worthy of double honor, especially those whose work is preaching and teaching."

Titus 1:5: "The reason I left you in Crete was that you might put in order what was left unfinished and appoint elders in every town, as I directed you."

○ **Overseers and leaders teach and equip the saints for maturity, ministry, and mission.**

Ephesians 4:11-12: "So Christ himself gave the apostles, the prophets, the evangelists, the pastors and teachers, to equip his people for works of service, so that the body of Christ may be built up."

James 3:1: "Not many of you should become teachers, my fellow believers, because you know that we who teach will be judged more strictly."

○ **Church discipline is exercised to guard the church and aid the individual believer.**

1 Corinthians 5:4-5: "So when you are assembled and I am with you in spirit, and the power of our Lord Jesus is present, hand this man over to Satan for the destruction of the flesh, so that his spirit may be saved on the day of the Lord."

6. **God's mission of disciple-making and servanthood are core priorities.**

○ **The church understands itself as an expression of God's kingdom mission.**

Matthew 6:9-10: "This, then, is how you should pray: 'Our Father in heaven, hallowed be your name, your kingdom come, your will be done, on earth as it is in heaven.'"

Matthew 6:33: "But seek first his kingdom and his righteousness, and all these things will be given to you as well."

○ **The Great Commission (going and making disciples) is prioritized and practiced.**

Matthew 28:19-20: "Therefore go and make disciples of all nations, baptizing them in the name of the Father and of the Son and of the Holy Spirit, and teaching them to obey everything I have commanded you. And surely I am with you always, to the very end of the age."

2 Timothy 2:2: "And the things you have heard me say in the presence of many witnesses entrust to reliable people who will also be qualified to teach others."

- **Serving in missional practices is prioritized and practiced.**

  Matthew 5:16: "In the same way, let your light shine before others, that they may see your good deeds and glorify your Father in heaven."

  1 Peter 2:12: "Live such good lives among the pagans that, though they accuse you of doing wrong, they may see your good deeds and glorify God on the day he visits us."

  Mark 10:45: "For even the Son of Man did not come to be served, but to serve, and to give his life as a ransom for many."

- **Evangelism is prioritized and viewed as the first step in disciple-making.**

  Acts 1:8: "But you will receive power when the Holy Spirit comes on you; and you will be my witnesses in Jerusalem, and in all Judea and Samaria, and to the ends of the earth."

  Acts 2:47: " ... praising God and enjoying the favor of all the people. And the Lord added to their number daily those who were being saved."

- **The priesthood of all believers shapes how the church pursues the mission.**

  Ephesians 2:10: "For we are God's handiwork, created in Christ Jesus to do good works, which God prepared in advance for us to do."

  1 Peter 2:9: "But you are a chosen people, a royal priesthood, a holy nation, God's special possession, that you may declare the praises of him who called you out of darkness into his wonderful light."

- **Intercessory prayer and fasting is practiced as a primary means of mission advancement.**

  Acts 2:42: "They devoted themselves to the apostles' teaching and to fellowship, to the breaking of bread and to prayer."

Colossians 4:3: "And pray for us, too, that God may open a door for our message, so that we may proclaim the mystery of Christ, for which I am in chains."

Acts 13:2: "While they were worshiping the Lord and fasting, the Holy Spirit said, 'Set apart for me Barnabas and Saul for the work to which I have called them.'"

7. **The presence of the Spirit is active in the gathering.**

1 Corinthians 12:13: "For we were all baptized by one Spirit so as to form one body — whether Jews or Gentiles, slave or free — and we were all given the one Spirit to drink."

1 Corinthians 3:16: "Don't you know that you yourselves are God's temple and that God's Spirit dwells in your midst?"

Acts 1:8: "But you will receive power when the Holy Spirit comes on you; and you will be my witnesses in Jerusalem, and in all Judea and Samaria, and to the ends of the earth."

Acts 2:4: "All of them were filled with the Holy Spirit ...."

- **The Spirit is empowering the fruit and gifts of the Spirit.**

  Galatians 5:22-23: "But the fruit of the Spirit is love, joy, peace, forbearance, kindness, goodness, faithfulness, gentleness and self-control. Against such things there is no law."

  1 Corinthians 12:7: "Now to each one the manifestation of the Spirit is given for the common good."

- **The Spirit is teaching the gathered believers.**

  John 14:26: "But the Advocate, the Holy Spirit, whom the Father will send in my name, will teach you all things and will remind you of everything I have said to you."

  1 John 2:27: "As for you, the anointing you received from him remains in you, and you do not need anyone to teach you. But as his anointing teaches you about all things and as that anointing is real, not counterfeit — just as it has taught you, remain in him."

○ **The Spirit is comforting and guiding the church.**

Acts 9:31: "Then the church throughout Judea, Galilee and Samaria enjoyed a time of peace and was strengthened. Living in the fear of the Lord and encouraged by the Holy Spirit, it increased in numbers."

ENDNOTES

1. While this book is written in Larry's voice, both Larry and Todd worked together on the conceptual framework for it.

2. http://www.built4ministry.com/mobilize.html.

3. *Oxford Dictionaries*, s.v. "flywheel," accessed Jan. 6, 2019, https://en.oxforddictionaries.com/definition/flywheel.

4. "The Flywheel Effect," Jim Collins, accessed Jan. 6, 2019, https://www.jimcollins.com/concepts/the-flywheel.html.

5. "Reinventing the (fly)wheel," *The Washington Post*, accessed Jan. 6, 2019, https://www.washingtonpost.com/national/science/reinventing-the-flywheel/2011/04/11/AFfd1J1D_story.html.

6. "Cyprian," Dan Graves, Christianity.com, accessed Jan. 6, 2019, https://www.christianity.com/church/church-history/timeline/1-300/cyprian-11629611.html.

7. Jean Calvin, *Calvin's Institutes* (Louisville: Westminster John Knox Press, 2000), 126.

8. "The Church, Our Mother," Journey with Jesus, accessed Jan. 6, 2019, https://www.journeywithjesus.net/Essays/20010507JJ.shtml.

9. Todd Wilson, Dave Ferguson, and Alan Hirsch, *Becoming a Level 5 Multiplying Church*, 34, https://exponential.org/resource-ebooks/becomingfive/.

10. "51% of Churchgoers Don't Know of the Great Commission," Barna, accessed Jan. 6, 2019, https://www.barna.com/research/half-churchgoers-not-heard-great-commission.

11. "Study: 64 percent of Christians Today Believe Evangelizing is Optional," ChristianHeadlines.com, accessed Jan. 6, 2019, https://www.christianheadlines.com/blog/study-64-percent-of-christians-today-believe-evangelizing-is-optional.html.

12. "The Holy Club," *Christianity Today*, accessed Jan. 6, 2019, https://www.christianitytoday.com/history/issues/issue-2/holy-club.html.

13. "Wesley's 'Methods' for Revival," Smallgroups.com, accessed Jan. 6, 2019, https://www.smallgroups.com/articles/1999/wesleys-methods-for-revival.html.

14. Julie Gorman, *Community That Is Christian* (Baker Books, 2002), 9.

15. "Americans Find Solace in Small Groups," Gallup, accessed Jan. 6, 2019, https://news.gallup.com/poll/5713/americans-find-solace-small-groups.aspx.

16. "How Well Do Today's Churches Make Disciples?" accessed Jan. 6, 2019, https://www.preachitteachit.org/articles/detail/how-well-do-todays-churches-make-disciples.

17. "Alan Hirsch, "The Forgotten Ways, and the future of the church in Europe," P.ost, accessed Jan. 6, 2019, https://www.postost.net/2008/03/alan-hirsch-forgotten-ways-future-church-europe.

18. "Reinventing the (fly)wheel," *The Washington Post*, accessed Jan. 6, 2019, https://www.washingtonpost.com/national/science/reinventing-the-flywheel/2011/04/11/AFfd1J1D_story.html.

19. https://en.wikipedia.org/wiki/A_rose_by_any_other_name_would_smell_as_sweet.

20. Used by permission of Ed Love, a Director of Church Planting for the Wesleyan Church.

21. "The Belgic Confession, 1561 (1619 version)," *Modern History Sourcebook*, Fordham University, accessed Jan. 6, 2019, https://sourcebooks.fordham.edu/mod/1562belgicconfession.asp, 2029.

22. "5 Truths for Church Planting Today: How to Be Effective in Disciple-Making in the Twenty-First Century," Volume 6, Issue 6, Lausanne Global Analysis, accessed Jan. 6, 2019, https://www.lausanne.org/content/lga/2017-11/5-truths-church-planting-today.

23. Dee W. Hock, *Birth of the Chaordic Age* (San Francisco: Bergen-Kuchler Publishers, 1999).

ABOUT THE AUTHORS

LARRY WALKEMEYER serves as the Lead Pastor of Light & Life Christian Fellowship in Long Beach, California. Starting with a handful of committed "white folks," the church has grown into a large multi-ethnic church, transforming its tough urban neighborhood. A priority on local and global church planting has led to the start of twenty-two churches nationally and dozens in Ethiopia, Philippines, and Indonesia.

As Director of Equipping and Spiritual Engagement for Exponential, Larry seeks to influence the church of Jesus toward multiplication. Holding a doctorate in church leadership and as the author of eight books (five for Exponential), Larry speaks and consults frequently. Azusa Pacific University has recognized Larry with the Centennial Award, naming him one of the most influential graduates in its history. Larry serves on the Board of Trustees for Azusa Pacific University.

Larry and Dr. Deb Walkemeyer have been married since 1978 and they write and speak frequently on marriage. They have two adult daughters. Larry enjoys snow skiing, waterskiing, biking, mission trips, and long walks on the beach.

TODD WILSON is co-founder and and CEO of Exponential (exponential.org), a community of activists devoted to church multiplication. The international organization's core focus is distributing resources for church multiplication leaders.

Todd earned a Bachelor of Science in nuclear engineering from North Carolina State University and a master's degree equivalent from the Bettis Atomic Power Laboratory. For fifteen years, he served in the Division of Naval Reactors on nuclear submarine design, operation, maintenance, and overhaul.

After a two-year wrestling match with God, Todd entered full-time vocational ministry as the Executive Pastor at New Life Christian Church, where he played a visionary and strategic role for several years as New Life grew and implemented key initiatives such as multisite, externally-focused outreach, and church planting. His passion for starting healthy new churches continues to grow. Todd now spends most of his energy engaged in a wide range of leading-edge and pioneering initiatives aimed at helping catalyze movements of healthy, multiplying churches.

Todd has written and co-written multiple books, including *Stories of Sifted* (with Eric Reiss), *Spark: Igniting a Culture of Multiplication, Becoming a Level Five Multiplying Church* (with Dave Ferguson), *More: Find Your Personal Calling and Live Life to the Fullest Measure* (Zondervan) *Dream Big, Plan Smart* (with Will Mancini), *Multipliers: Leading Beyond Addition, The Legacy of a Hero Maker* (with Dave Ferguson), and *Made for More* (with Rob Wegner).

Todd is married to Anna, and they have two adult sons who are both married — Ben to Therese and Chris to Mariah.

Made in the USA
Middletown, DE
18 April 2019